QUICK FROM SCRATCH
One-Dish Meals

Rice with Mozzarella, Prosciutto, and Peas, page 51

QUICK FROM SCRATCH
One-Dish Meals

American Express Publishing Corporation
New York

Editor in Chief: Judith Hill
Associate Editor: Susan Lantzius
Assistant Editor: Laura Byrne Russell
Managing Editor: Terri Mauro
Copy Editor: Barbara A. Mateer
Wine Editor: Steve Miller
Recipe Consultant: Judith Sutton
Art Director: Nina Scerbo
Editorial Assistant: Evette Manners
Photographer: Melanie Acevedo
Food Stylist: Rori Spinelli
Prop Stylist: Robyn Glaser
Production Manager: Yvette Williams-Braxton

Vice President, Books and Information Services: John Stoops
Marketing Director: David Geller
Marketing/Promotion Manager: Roni Stein
Operations Manager: Doreen Camardi
Business Manager: Joanne Ragazzo

Recipes Pictured on Cover: (Front) Lamb Fattoush, page 177
(Back) Spaghetti with Grilled Shrimp, Zucchini, and Salsa Verde, page 21;
Inset top: Salmon-and-Corn Chowder with Lima Beans, page 71;
Inset bottom: Chicken Chilaquiles, page 123
Page 6: *Kitchen photo:* Bill Bettencourt; *Portraits:* Christopher Dinerman

AMERICAN EXPRESS PUBLISHING CORPORATION
©1997 American Express Publishing Corporation

LIBRARY OF CONGRESS CATALOGING-IN-PUBLICATION DATA
Quick from scratch. One-Dish Meals.
p.   cm.
Includes index.
ISBN 0-916103-40-4
1. Entrées (Cookery) 2. Quick and easy cookery. I. Food & wine (New York, N.Y.)
TX740.Q524   1997

TX740.Q524   97-33650
641.8'2—dc21   CIP

Published by American Express Publishing Corporation
1120 Avenue of the Americas, New York, New York 10036

Manufactured in the United States of America

CONTENTS

RECIPES PICTURED ABOVE: (*left to right*) pages 173, 57, 121

A one-dish meal passes the taste test in the FOOD & WINE Books kitchen.

Susan Lantzius trained at La Varenne École de Cuisine in Paris, worked as a chef in Portugal for a year, and then headed to New York City. There she made her mark first as head decorator at the well-known Sant Ambroeus pastry shop and next as a pastry chef, working at such top restaurants as San Domenico and Maxim's. In 1993, she turned her talents to recipe development and editorial work for FOOD & WINE Books.

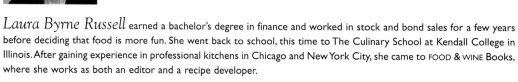

Judith Hill is the editor in chief of FOOD & WINE Books, a division of American Express Publishing. Previously she was editor in chief of COOK'S Magazine, director of publications for La Varenne École de Cuisine in Paris, from which she earned a Grand Diplôme, and an English instructor for the University of Maryland International Division in Germany. Her book credits include editing cookbooks for Fredy Girardet, Jane Grigson, Michel Guérard, and Anne Willan.

Laura Byrne Russell earned a bachelor's degree in finance and worked in stock and bond sales for a few years before deciding that food is more fun. She went back to school, this time to The Culinary School at Kendall College in Illinois. After gaining experience in professional kitchens in Chicago and New York City, she came to FOOD & WINE Books, where she works as both an editor and a recipe developer.

INTRODUCTION

When I was growing up, my family ate dinner together every evening. Our plates typically held three separately prepared dishes: a meat, a starch, and a vegetable. Susan Lantzius and Laura Russell, the combination editor/recipe developers who planned this book with me, report exactly the same thing. Laura and I each continued our family's agreeable model in our own marriages . . . for a while, that is. More recently, we and our spouses get home late and tired and don't even want to think about making more than one dish. Susan and her husband *do* make a big meal, including separate meat, starch, and vegetable, most nights, but she says, "Oh, don't count us as normal. We're newlyweds." Laura and I give them a year tops before they change their routine.

I doubt that we're unusual in this tendency to streamline. Today's schedules make everyone lean more and more toward one-dish meals, perhaps pasta with both vegetables and a protein in the sauce, or a big salad with meat or cheese in addition to the greens and either croutons or just bread on the side. Even when each element that goes into a single dish takes a little preparation, something about focusing on producing just one main thing to eat seems to make a meal more manageable.

Despite our schedules, we do want to dine together with our spouses or families at the end of even the busiest weekday, and we want to eat well. That's what this volume of *Quick from Scratch* is all about: good, doable dishes that include the three major components of a traditional American meal. You'll find lots of ideas both homegrown and internationally inspired, from gumbo to curry, from savory bread pudding to French gratins, from po' boys to calzone.

We hope you'll use many of these recipes, just one at a time. Make a dish, pour a glass of wine, and relax over dinner.

Judith Hill
Editor in Chief
FOOD & WINE Books

Before You Begin

You'll find test-kitchen tips and ideas for ingredient substitutions presented with the individual recipes throughout the book. In this opening section, we've gathered information and tips that apply to all, or at least a substantial number, of the recipes. These are the facts and opinions that we'd like you to know before you use the recipes and to keep in mind while you use them. We hope you'll read these pages prior to cooking from the book for the first time. The culinary information here will help make your cooking quicker, simpler, more inventive, and tastier.

MAKING YOUR OWN ONE-DISH MEALS

At the fingertips of every hurried weeknight cook is a one-dish meal waiting to be created. Use our recipes as guides and come up with your own combinations based on what you feel like eating or happen to have on hand. Choose at least one from each column.

STARCH	+	PROTEIN	+	VEGETABLES	+	ENHANCERS	=	FINAL DISH
Bread		Cheese		Anything fresh		Capers		
Couscous		Eggs				Citrus juice		
Legumes		Meat		Frozen peas, corn, okra, lima beans, or spinach		Garlic		
Pasta		Nuts				Herbs		
Polenta		Poultry				Mustard		
Potatoes		Seafood		Sun-dried tomatoes		Olives		
Rice		Tofu				Spices		
						Zest		

For example:

	+		+		+		=	
Rice		Crab		Asparagus		Orange zest Parsley Garlic		Asparagus Risotto with Crab and Orange Gremolada, page 41
Bread		Pork Chops		Mushrooms		Thyme		Pork Chops with Mushroom Bread Pudding, page 97

RECIPES PICTURED OPPOSITE: (top) pages 61, 175, 31; (center) pages 23, 51, 117; (bottom) pages 71, 177, 145

ESSENTIAL INGREDIENT INFORMATION

Broth, Chicken

We tested the recipes in this book with canned low-sodium chicken broth. You can almost always substitute regular for low-sodium broth; just cut back on the salt in the recipe. And if you keep homemade stock in your freezer, by all means feel free to use it. We aren't suggesting that it won't work as well, only that we know the dishes taste delicious even when made with canned broth.

Butter

Our recipes don't specify whether to use salted or unsalted butter. We generally use unsalted, but in these savory dishes, it really won't make a big difference which type you use.

Citrus Juice

Many of our recipes call for lemon or lime juice. For a bright boost of flavor, use juice from fresh fruit. The bottled stuff just doesn't taste as good.

Coconut Milk

Coconut milk is the traditional liquid used in many Thai and Indian curries. Make sure you buy *unsweetened* canned coconut milk, not cream of coconut, which is used primarily for piña coladas. Heavy cream can be substituted in many recipes.

Garlic

The size of garlic cloves varies tremendously. When we call for one minced or chopped clove, we expect you to get about three-quarters of a teaspoon.

Ginger, Fresh

Fresh ginger, or ginger root, is a knobby, tan-skinned rhizome found in the produce section of your supermarket. You need to peel its thin skin before using; this is most easily accomplished by scraping it with a spoon. After peeling, the ginger is ready to be grated, sliced, or chopped.

Mustard

When we call for mustard, we mean Dijon or grainy. We never, ever mean yellow ballpark mustard.

Nuts

Our quick pantry wouldn't be complete without several kinds of nuts. Keep in mind that nuts have a high percentage of oil and can turn rancid quickly. We store ours in the freezer to keep them fresh.

Oil

Cooking oil in these recipes refers to readily available, reasonably priced nut, seed, or vegetable oil with a high smoking point, such as peanut, sunflower, canola, safflower, or corn oil. These can be heated to about 400° before they begin to smoke, break down, and develop an unpleasant flavor.

Parsley

Many of our recipes call for chopped fresh parsley. The flat-leaf variety has a stronger flavor than the curly, and we use it most of the time, but unless the type is specified, you can use either.

Pepper

■ There's nothing like fresh-ground pepper. If you've been using preground, buy a pepper mill, fill it, and give it a grind. You'll never look back.

■ To measure your just-ground pepper more easily, become familiar with your own mill; each produces a different amount per turn. You'll probably find that ten to fifteen grinds produces one-quarter teaspoon of pepper, and then you can count on that forever after.

Tomatoes, Canned

In some recipes, we call for "crushed tomatoes in thick puree." Depending on the brand, this mix of crushed tomatoes and tomato puree may be labeled crushed tomatoes with puree, with added puree, in tomato puree, thick style, or in thick puree. You can use any of these.

Wine, Dry White

Leftover wine is ideal for cooking. It seems a shame to open a fresh bottle for just a few spoonfuls. Another solution is to keep dry vermouth on hand. You can use whatever quantity is needed; the rest will keep indefinitely.

Zest

Citrus zest—the colored part of the peel, without any white pith—adds tremendous flavor to many a dish. Remove the zest from the fruit using either a grater or a zester. A zester is a small, inexpensive, and extremely handy tool. It has little holes that remove just the zest in fine ribbons. A zester is quick, easy to clean, and never scrapes your knuckles.

Faster, Better, Easier
TEST-KITCHEN TIPS

Improving fresh tomatoes

Since it's increasingly difficult to find ripe, delicious tomatoes, we often salt ours to remove some of the moisture. This trick intensifies the flavor. (Taken to the extreme, the dehydrating trick yields dried tomatoes, which deliver a *much* stronger taste than fresh.) Just slice or dice your tomatoes, toss them with a little salt, and let them drain in a strainer or on paper towels for about 15 minutes.

The cardinal rules of browning

■ To get a good brown crust when sautéing meat, poultry, or fish, the first essential is to start with hot oil in a hot pan. You should hear a strong sizzle as the food hits the oil. The sound of silence means the oil's too cold and the food is sitting in the pan stewing.

■ Use a pan large enough to hold all the pieces with at least half an inch between them. When too much food is put in the pan at once, the temperature of the pan and the oil drops and again, the pieces stew rather than brown. If your pan isn't big enough, brown in batches.

■ Remember to pat food dry before sautéing. Any excess moisture will cause spattering and inhibit browning.

Juicy meat in soups

Bite-size pieces of tender fish, meat, and chicken need only a few minutes in the soup pot to cook completely; any longer, and they become dry and stringy. If you're making soup ahead of time, you can avoid overcooking by waiting to add these ingredients until you reheat the soup just before serving.

Shredding fresh herbs

Shredding herbs with large leaves, such as basil, mint, or sage, can be accomplished quickly by stacking several leaves on top of one another, rolling them up like a cigar, and then cutting them crosswise into thin slices. You'll have a pile of sliced herbs in no time.

Chicken stock

Keep a plastic bag in your freezer to store extra chicken wings, necks, backs, and gizzards as you accumulate them from other recipes. Then enhance canned broth by simmering it with a few of these chicken pieces for about fifteen minutes. This will add a surprising amount of flavor. Or keep stockpiling the chicken parts until you've got enough to make a batch of homemade stock. Freeze the stock in small containers so you'll always have some on hand.

Adjusting the thickness of soups, stews, or sauces

Depending on your stove, the diameter of your pans, and any number of other factors, you may follow a recipe to the letter and end up with a dish that isn't as thick or thin as anticipated. To thicken, take the lid off the pot, bring the liquid to a boil, and let excess moisture evaporate until the soup or sauce is the consistency you like. (Remove the meat, fish, or chicken first to avoid overcooking.) Thinning is even easier. Simply add a little water or more of the liquid component of the dish, such as chicken stock or wine.

Keeping fresh ginger

We use fresh ginger in numerous dishes because of its distinctive flavor. It is not interchangeable with powdered ginger, which is a fine spice but tastes almost entirely different. For easy access, keep a bulb of ginger root in your refrigerator for a few weeks or in the freezer. You can peel and grate a small portion of ginger when you need it. Frozen ginger is easy to peel and the heat of your hands is usually enough to thaw it for grating.

The fastest way to peel garlic

To peel a garlic clove, put the flat of the blade of a large knife over the garlic and smack the blade with your fist or the heel of your hand. The clove will crack, and the skin will loosen and come off easily. If you like gadgets, try one of the garlic peelers that looks like a piece of rubber hose. They work well, too.

Nonstick pans

Occasionally, we specify using a nonstick pan, which comes in handy when cooking delicate ingredients, such as fish fillets, or those with a tendency to stick. If you don't have a nonstick pan, you may need to increase the amount of cooking fat in the recipe by a tablespoon or two. Also, shake the pan every now and then to discourage sticking.

Foolproof rice

Steaming rice can be a guess-and-hope affair: The amount of water and time needed vary according to the type of rice, how fresh it is, even the humidity in the air. For foolproof rice, boil it in a lot of salted water just as you do pasta. Test a grain occasionally; most rice takes about fifteen minutes. When the rice is done, drain it, return it to the pot, and cover to keep warm.

Salting water

We always cook pasta and blanch vegetables in boiling, salted water. This step is essential for a well-seasoned dish. The salty water penetrates and becomes part of the food. No amount of salting at the table can make up for insufficient seasoning while cooking. Count on using about one-and-a-half tablespoons of salt for every three quarts of water. Taste the water; if it doesn't taste like anything, neither will your food.

CHAPTER ONE

Pasta

WHOLE-WHEAT PASTA WITH TOFU AND CUCUMBER

An updated pasta salad—whole-wheat spaghetti served at room temperature with sautéed tofu, cucumbers, scallions, and an Asian dressing—makes a delicious warm-weather meal, reminiscent of Japanese soba-noodle dishes.

WINE RECOMMENDATION

The crisp citrus tang of a German riesling spätlese halbtrocken is just right for this summery dish and its Asian flavors. *Halbtrocken* means half dry, or just a little sweet. Try one from the Pfalz, where the sunny climate yields fruity wines.

SERVES 4

¾ pound whole-wheat spaghetti

1¼ pounds firm tofu, cut into ½-inch dice

1 tablespoon plus 4 teaspoons soy sauce

2½ teaspoons grated fresh ginger

2½ tablespoons cooking oil

2 tablespoons wine vinegar

1½ teaspoons lemon juice

1 teaspoon Asian sesame oil

¾ teaspoon grated lemon zest

¼ teaspoon salt

⅛ teaspoon cayenne

2 cucumbers, peeled, halved lengthwise, seeded, and cut into ¼-inch slices

3 scallions including green tops, sliced

3 tablespoons chopped cilantro or fresh parsley

1. In a large pot of boiling, salted water, cook the spaghetti until just done, about 15 minutes. Drain the pasta. Rinse with cold water and drain thoroughly.

2. In a medium bowl, combine the tofu with the 1 tablespoon soy sauce and ½ teaspoon of the grated ginger. Let sit for about 5 minutes.

3. In a large glass or stainless-steel bowl, combine the remaining 2 teaspoons ginger and 4 teaspoons soy sauce, 1½ tablespoons of the cooking oil, the vinegar, lemon juice, sesame oil, lemon zest, salt, and cayenne.

4. In a large nonstick frying pan, heat the remaining 1 tablespoon cooking oil over moderate heat. Add the tofu and cook, stirring frequently, until browned, about 8 minutes. Add the tofu, pasta, cucumbers, scallions, and cilantro to the dressing in the large bowl and toss.

FUSILLI WITH THREE CHEESES AND RED BELL PEPPER

Macaroni and cheese goes upscale with fontina, mozzarella, and Parmesan. This particular combination provides plenty of flavor and meltability, but don't limit yourself to our selection: Make your own trio from the cheeses you have on hand.

WINE RECOMMENDATION
Creamy cheeses need a light red wine as a foil for their richness. A weighty Chianti Classico or Riserva would be overpowering here, but a basic Chianti, with its slight bitter-cherry flavor, will strike just the right balance.

SERVES 4

4	tablespoons butter
2	red bell peppers, cut into thin strips
1	teaspoon salt
¾	pound fusilli
¼	pound fontina, grated (about 1 cup)
3	ounces mozzarella, grated (about ¾ cup)
6	tablespoons grated Parmesan, plus more for serving
¼	teaspoon fresh-ground black pepper

1. In a medium frying pan, melt one tablespoon of the butter over moderately low heat. Add the bell peppers and ¼ teaspoon of the salt and cook until soft, about 10 minutes.

2. Heat the broiler. Butter a large shallow baking dish.

3. In a large pot of boiling, salted water, cook the fusilli until just done, about 13 minutes. Drain and return to the hot pot. Toss the pasta with the remaining 3 tablespoons butter and ¾ teaspoon salt, the sautéed bell peppers, the fontina, mozzarella, 3 tablespoons of the Parmesan, and the black pepper.

4. Transfer the pasta to the prepared baking dish and sprinkle the remaining 3 tablespoons Parmesan over the top. Broil until the top starts to brown, 3 to 4 minutes. Serve with additional Parmesan.

BROWNED AND BUBBLING

Cheese often turns stringy when tossed with hot pasta. Broiling the dish after tossing melts the strings into a smooth sauce. An added bonus: that irresistible brown crust.

Spaghetti with Grilled Shrimp, Zucchini, and Salsa Verde

Summer is the perfect time for this colorful pasta—zucchini is in abundance, and recipes that make good use of the outdoor grill are in demand. Both the squash and the shrimp here take their turn on the coals before being tossed with the spaghetti. If you crave the dish in the winter, cook the zucchini and shrimp in the broiler.

WINE RECOMMENDATION
Sauvignon blanc has a great affinity for the flavors of lemon and mustard. To complement the richness of the pasta and shrimp, go for a vibrant Pouilly-Fumé from France's Loire Valley. A Sancerre will work almost as well.

SERVES 4

⅔ cup lightly packed parsley leaves

3 tablespoons drained capers

1 clove garlic, chopped

4 teaspoons lemon juice

1 teaspoon anchovy paste

½ teaspoon Dijon mustard

1¼ teaspoons salt

¼ teaspoon fresh-ground black pepper

½ cup plus 2 tablespoons olive oil

2 zucchini, cut lengthwise into ¼-inch slices

1¼ pounds large shrimp, shelled

¾ pound spaghetti

1. Put the parsley, capers, garlic, lemon juice, anchovy paste, mustard, ½ teaspoon of the salt, and the pepper into a food processor or blender. Pulse just to chop, six to eight times. With the machine running, add the ½ cup oil in a thin stream to make a coarse puree. Leave this salsa verde in the food processor; if necessary, pulse to re-emulsify just before adding to the pasta.

2. Light the grill or heat the broiler. Brush the zucchini with 1 tablespoon of the oil and sprinkle with ¼ teaspoon of the salt. Grill or broil the zucchini, turning, until just done, about 10 minutes in all. When the slices are cool enough to handle, cut them crosswise into ½-inch pieces and put them in a large bowl.

3. Thread the shrimp onto skewers. Brush the shrimp with the remaining 1 tablespoon oil and sprinkle with the remaining ½ teaspoon salt. Grill or broil the shrimp, turning, until just done, about 4 minutes in all. Remove the shrimp from the skewers, slice them in half horizontally, and add them to the zucchini.

4. Meanwhile, in a large pot of boiling, salted water, cook the spaghetti until just done, about 12 minutes. Drain. Add the pasta to the grilled zucchini and shrimp and toss with the salsa verde.

LINGUINE WITH SCALLOPS, SUN-DRIED TOMATOES, AND PINE NUTS

Sweet scallops, intense sun-dried tomatoes, and rich, crunchy pine nuts offer a rather incredible blend of textures and flavors. Don't cook the scallops too long or they'll toughen. If you have bay rather than sea scallops, use them whole and sauté them, stirring, for no more than two minutes in all.

WINE RECOMMENDATION

Many think tocai friulano is northeastern Italy's finest white wine. Full and rich enough to partner the scallops, it also has enough crisp acidity to stand up to the tomatoes. The wine's nutty taste makes it a natural with this dish.

SERVES 4

¼ cup pine nuts

¾ pound linguine

6 tablespoons olive oil

1½ pounds sea scallops

   Salt

½ cup drained oil-packed sun-dried tomatoes, cut into ¼-inch pieces

6 cloves garlic, minced

6 tablespoons chopped fresh parsley

   Scant ½ teaspoon dried red-pepper flakes

1. Heat the oven to 350°. Toast the pine nuts in the oven until golden brown, about 8 minutes.

2. In a large pot of boiling, salted water, cook the linguine until just done, about 12 minutes. Drain the pasta.

3. Meanwhile, heat 1 tablespoon of the oil in a large nonstick frying pan over moderately high heat until very hot. Season the scallops with ⅛ teaspoon salt. Put the scallops in the pan and sear until brown on the bottom, 1 to 2 minutes. Turn and sear until brown on the other side, 1 to 2 minutes longer. Remove the scallops and cut them into quarters.

4. In the same pan, heat the remaining 5 tablespoons oil over moderate heat. Add the tomatoes, garlic, 2 tablespoons of the parsley, the red-pepper flakes, and ½ teaspoon salt. Cook, stirring, for 1 minute. Toss with the pasta, scallops, pine nuts, and the remaining 4 tablespoons of parsley.

RECONSTITUTING DRY-PACKED SUN-DRIED TOMATOES

You can use dry-packed tomatoes in place of the oil-packed ones. To reconstitute, put them in a bowl with boiling water to cover well. Let sit for five minutes and then drain.

LINGUINE WITH TUNA, CAPERS, AND OLIVES

When it comes to making quick, delicious pasta sauces, Italians hold canned tuna in high regard. We complement it with Provençal herbs and orange zest. If you're a lemon-zest fan, try that instead of the orange.

WINE RECOMMENDATION

A robust French rosé from the southern Rhône appellation of Tavel will serve these Mediterranean ingredients well. Earthy and full of roasted raspberry flavor, Tavels are among the most full-bodied of rosés. If you'd rather stick to the Italian theme, look for the wonderful Sicilian rosé from Regaleali.

SERVES 4

- 2 tablespoons olive oil
- 3 cloves garlic, minced
- 1/4 teaspoon dried sage
- 1/4 teaspoon dried rosemary
- 3/4 teaspoon grated orange zest (from 1/2 orange)
- 1 tablespoon drained chopped capers
- 1/4 cup chopped green olives
- 1/2 teaspoon salt
- 1/4 teaspoon fresh-ground black pepper
- 2 6-ounce cans tuna packed in olive oil
- 1/2 teaspoon wine vinegar
- 3/4 pound linguine
- 2 tablespoons chopped fresh parsley

1. In a medium frying pan, heat the oil over moderately low heat. Add the garlic, sage, and rosemary and stir until the garlic just starts to brown, 2 to 3 minutes. Stir in the orange zest, capers, olives, salt, pepper, and the tuna with its oil. Remove from the heat; stir in the vinegar.

2. In a large pot of boiling, salted water, cook the linguine until just done, about 12 minutes. Drain the pasta and toss with the tuna sauce and parsley.

TUNA PACKED IN OIL

Here we use tuna packed in olive oil, and we count on that oil as part of the sauce. If your tuna doesn't have at least one-and-a-half tablespoons of oil per can, add a little more olive oil to make up the difference. Of course, you can use tuna packed in vegetable oil, too, but avoid water-packed tuna at all costs. The flavor, and most of the nutrients for that matter, leach out into the water.

ORZO WITH CHICKEN, RED PEPPER, AND SHIITAKES

With its rice-shaped orzo and creamy texture, this pasta may remind you of risotto—but it's easier to make, since you don't have to stir and stir and stir.

WINE RECOMMENDATION
Sauvignon-blanc-based wines go particularly well with goat cheese, and a piquant Sancerre, with its grassy currant and gooseberry fruit, will make this dish sing.

SERVES 4

- 5 tablespoons olive oil
- 1⅓ pounds boneless, skinless chicken breasts (about 4 in all)
- Salt
- Fresh-ground black pepper
- 1 red bell pepper, cut into ½-inch pieces
- ¼ pound shiitake mushrooms, stems removed, caps cut into ¼-inch slices
- ½ teaspoon dried thyme
- 2 cloves garlic, minced
- 1 pound orzo
- ¼ pound mild goat cheese, such as Montrachet
- ⅓ cup heavy cream
- ¼ cup chopped fresh parsley

1. In a large nonstick frying pan, heat 1 tablespoon of the oil over moderate heat. Season the chicken with ¼ teaspoon salt and ⅛ teaspoon black pepper. Put the chicken in the pan and cook for 5 minutes. Turn and cook until just done, about 5 minutes longer. Remove. When the chicken is cool enough to handle, cut the breasts crosswise into ¼-inch slices.

2. Heat 2 tablespoons of the oil in the same pan over moderately high heat. Put in the bell pepper, shiitakes, thyme, and ⅛ teaspoon salt. Cook, stirring frequently, until the mushrooms are golden brown, about 5 minutes. Add the garlic and cook, stirring, for 30 seconds longer. Remove from the heat.

3. In a large pot of boiling, salted water, cook the orzo until just done, about 12 minutes. Reserve ½ cup of the pasta water; drain the orzo.

4. In the frying pan, combine the reserved pasta water with the remaining 2 tablespoons oil, the goat cheese, cream, ¾ teaspoon salt, and ¼ teaspoon pepper. Bring almost to a simmer over moderate heat, stirring, until smooth, about 2 minutes. Add the orzo, chicken, and 3 tablespoons of the parsley and stir to combine. Serve topped with the remaining 1 tablespoon parsley.

VERMICELLI WITH CHICKEN SKEWERS AND NUOC CHAM

In this version of a Vietnamese dish, individual piles of cucumber, fresh herbs, and grilled chicken are arranged on a platter of vermicelli and bean sprouts. Tangy *nuoc cham* sauce is poured over all. As each diner takes a portion, the components intermingle.

WINE RECOMMENDATION
The high acidity, citrus and mineral flavors, and slight sweetness of a German riesling are the perfect foils for the sweet and savory taste of this dish. Try a young kabinett from the Mosel region.

SERVES 4

- 5 tablespoons Asian fish sauce (nuoc mam or nam pla)*
- 2 tablespoons sugar
- 3 cloves garlic, minced
- 1 tablespoon cooking oil
- 1 pound boneless, skinless chicken breasts (about 3), cut lengthwise into 12 strips in all
- ½ teaspoon dried red-pepper flakes
- 1 teaspoon wine vinegar
- 2 tablespoons plus 1 teaspoon lime juice (from about 2 limes)
- 2 tablespoons water
- ½ pound vermicelli
- 1 cup bean sprouts
- 1 cucumber, peeled, halved lengthwise, seeded, and cut into thin slices
- ⅔ cup fresh mint, basil, or cilantro leaves, or any combination of the three
- ⅓ cup chopped peanuts

  *Available at Asian markets and many supermarkets

1. Heat the broiler or light the grill. In a medium bowl, combine 1 tablespoon of the fish sauce, 1 tablespoon of the sugar, 2 cloves of the garlic, and the oil. Add the chicken, toss, and then thread each strip onto a wooden skewer. Broil or grill the chicken until just done, about 2 minutes per side.

2. In a small bowl, combine the remaining 4 tablespoons fish sauce, 1 tablespoon sugar, and 1 clove garlic with the red-pepper flakes, vinegar, lime juice, and water. Set this *nuoc cham* aside.

3. In a pot of boiling, salted water, cook the vermicelli until just done, about 9 minutes. Add the bean sprouts during the last minute of cooking. Drain, rinse with cold water, and drain thoroughly.

4. Put the pasta and bean sprouts on a platter and top with the cucumber, herbs, and chicken skewers. Pour the *nuoc cham* over all and sprinkle with the peanuts.

COUNTRY-STYLE RIGATONI

Sausage, escarole, and white beans join chunky rigatoni in a garlicky broth slightly thickened with Parmesan. Don't stir too much after adding the beans, or they'll break up.

WINE RECOMMENDATION
This simple country-style pasta will be right at home with a rustic red from Italy. Go for a flavor-packed but surprisingly inexpensive Salice Salentino from Apulia, the hot, sunny heel of Italy's boot.

SERVES 4

1   tablespoon cooking oil

1   pound mild or hot Italian sausage

3   cloves garlic, minced

2   cups canned low-sodium chicken broth or homemade stock

1   head escarole, torn into 2-inch pieces (about 2 quarts)

1   cup drained and rinsed canned cannellini beans (from one 15-ounce can)

1/3   cup grated Parmesan, plus more for serving

1/2   teaspoon salt

1/4   teaspoon fresh-ground black pepper

3/4   pound rigatoni

1. In a large deep frying pan, heat the oil over moderate heat. Add the sausage and cook, turning, until browned and cooked through, about 10 minutes. Remove. When the sausage is cool enough to handle, cut it into slices.

2. Put the garlic and the broth in the pan and bring to a simmer. Add the escarole, cover, and simmer for 5 minutes. Gently stir in the sausage, beans, Parmesan, salt, and pepper and simmer 1 minute longer.

3. Meanwhile, in a large pot of boiling, salted water, cook the pasta until just done, about 14 minutes. Drain and toss with the sauce. Serve with additional Parmesan.

BEST BEANS

Many canned beans are overcooked during processing to the point of mush. We find, though, that the Goya company consistently delivers a nice firm bean that holds up to reheating without falling apart.

CAVATELLI WITH BACON AND ARUGULA

A quick tomato sauce dresses chewy cavatelli, crisp bacon, and peppery arugula. Be sure to add the arugula at the last minute; if it actually cooks, it may turn bitter.

WINE RECOMMENDATION
Barbera is unique among Italian reds in that it is fruity and very high in acid, yet has almost no tannins. These qualities make the wine remarkably adaptable to food, particularly tomatoes. Try an unoaked Barbera d'Alba for a delicious match here.

SERVES 4

¼ pound sliced bacon, cut crosswise into ½-inch strips

1 onion, chopped

1¾ cups canned crushed tomatoes (one 15-ounce can)

¾ teaspoon salt

¼ teaspoon fresh-ground black pepper

1 pound frozen cavatelli

1¼ cups arugula, stems removed, leaves torn in half (one 2-ounce bunch)

⅓ cup grated Parmesan

1. In a large stainless-steel frying pan, cook the bacon over moderate heat until almost crisp. Remove with a slotted spoon. Pour off all but 1 tablespoon of the fat from the pan.

2. Reduce the heat to moderately low. Add the onion and cook, stirring occasionally, until soft, about 5 minutes. Add the tomatoes with their juice, the salt, and the pepper and bring to a simmer. Cover and cook for 10 minutes.

3. In a large pot of boiling, salted water, cook the cavatelli until just done, about 10 minutes. Drain and toss with the sauce, bacon, arugula, and ¼ cup of the Parmesan. Stir until the arugula just wilts. Sprinkle the remaining Parmesan over the top.

VARIATIONS

Use 1¼ cups **watercress** or **spinach**, large stems removed, instead of the arugula.

CAVATELLI OPTIONS

Look for cavatelli in the frozen-foods section of your grocery store. If you prefer, substitute frozen egg noodles or gnocchi in equal amounts for the cavatelli; they have a similar doughy chew. This dish could also be made successfully with spaghetti or, even better, spaghettini.

Tortellini with Ham, Peas, and Tomato Cream Sauce

You'll be surprised how easy it is to make this creamy tomato sauce that is so popular in Italian restaurants. If you prefer, replace the cheese tortellini with mushroom- or meat-filled pasta of any shape.

WINE RECOMMENDATION
A light, fruity, and very crisp Italian red will cut the sauce's creaminess and refresh the palate. Valpolicella is a perfect choice. For a treat, bypass the well-known commercial brands and seek out a Valpolicella Classico from a small estate.

SERVES 4

2 tablespoons butter

1 onion, chopped

2½ cups canned crushed tomatoes (from one 28-ounce can)

1 teaspoon salt

¼ teaspoon fresh-ground black pepper

½ cup heavy cream

1 pound cheese tortellini

¼ pound ham, cut into ¼-inch dice

¾ cup frozen petite peas, defrosted

1. In a large stainless-steel frying pan, melt the butter over moderately low heat. Add the onion; cook, stirring occasionally, until starting to soften, about 3 minutes. Stir in the tomatoes with their juice, the salt, and the pepper. Simmer for 10 minutes. Add the cream and cook for 1 minute longer.

2. Meanwhile, in a large pot of boiling, salted water, cook the tortellini until just done, about 4 minutes for fresh, 12 minutes for frozen. Drain the pasta and add it to the pan with the sauce. Stir in the ham and peas and cook until warmed through, about 2 minutes.

Variations

■ Substitute ¼ pound sliced **prosciutto**, cut into thin strips, for the ham.

■ Stir in ¼ cup **fresh basil leaves**, cut into thin strips, with the ham and peas.

BAKED SHELLS WITH PESTO, MOZZARELLA, AND MEAT SAUCE

Here's a true crowd pleaser: pasta shells in a simple sauce of ground beef, tomatoes, and pesto, layered with mozzarella and Parmesan and baked until bubbly. Fusilli or orecchiette would work well here, too.

WINE RECOMMENDATION
This robust dish with its meat and tomatoes calls for a gutsy red wine from Italy. A Chianti Classico Riserva's medium body, dried-cherry flavor, high acidity, and moderate tannins will fill the bill perfectly.

SERVES 4

1 tablespoon cooking oil

1 onion, chopped

1 pound ground beef

2 cups canned chopped tomatoes, drained (from one 28-ounce can)

1½ teaspoons salt

½ cup store-bought or homemade pesto

¾ pound medium pasta shells

6 ounces mozzarella, grated (about 1½ cups)

¼ cup grated Parmesan

1. Heat the oven to 400°. Oil a large baking dish (about 9 by 13 inches).

2. In a large stainless-steel frying pan, heat the oil over moderately low heat. Add the onion and cook, stirring occasionally, until starting to soften, about 3 minutes. Stir in the ground beef and cook, breaking it up, until the meat is no longer pink, about 2 minutes. Drain off any excess fat.

3. Add the tomatoes and salt to the pan and bring to a simmer. Cook until most of the liquid evaporates, about 10 minutes. Remove the pan from the heat and stir in the pesto.

4. Meanwhile, in a large pot of boiling, salted water, cook the shells until just done, about 10 minutes. Drain and toss with the sauce. Put half of the pasta into the prepared baking dish and top with half the mozzarella and 2 tablespoons of the Parmesan. Repeat with the remaining pasta, mozzarella, and Parmesan. Bake until bubbling, about 15 minutes.

VARIATION

Almost any relatively soft, mild cheese will taste good here. You might try **fontina** in place of the mozzarella, or even **Gouda** or **Havarti**.

CHAPTER TWO

Rice, Couscous & Polenta

ASPARAGUS RISOTTO WITH CRAB AND ORANGE GREMOLADA

Crabmeat and asparagus is a match made in heaven. This recipe is also fantastic, however, without any crab at all. Leave it out and serve the risotto as a side dish or as a first course at a springtime dinner party.

WINE RECOMMENDATION
Asparagus is hard to pair with wine; it combines with any bitter elements to produce a metallic taste. That means no tannins and definitely no oak. Go for a crisp, unoaked Italian sauvignon blanc from Friuli or Collio.

SERVES 4

1 quart canned low-sodium chicken broth or homemade stock, more if needed

1½ cups water, more if needed

1 pound asparagus, tough ends snapped off and discarded, spears cut into ½-inch lengths, tips left whole

2 tablespoons butter

1 tablespoon cooking oil

1 small onion, chopped

1½ cups arborio rice

½ cup dry vermouth or dry white wine

1¼ teaspoons salt

½ pound crabmeat, picked free of shell

1 teaspoon grated orange zest (from ½ orange)

2 cloves garlic, minced

¼ cup chopped fresh parsley

¼ teaspoon fresh-ground black pepper

1. Bring the broth and water to a simmer in a medium pot. Cook the asparagus in the broth until just done, about 4 minutes. Remove with a slotted spoon. Put in a colander, rinse with cold water, and drain. Keep the broth at a simmer.

2. In a large pot, melt 1 tablespoon of the butter with the oil. Add the onion and cook, stirring occasionally, until translucent, about 5 minutes. Add the rice and stir until it begins to turn opaque, about 2 minutes.

3. Add the vermouth and salt. Cook, stirring, until the vermouth is absorbed. Add about ½ cup of the simmering broth; cook, stirring frequently, until absorbed. The rice and broth should bubble gently; adjust the heat as needed. Continue cooking, adding broth ½ cup at a time and letting the rice absorb it before adding more. Cook the rice in this way until tender, 25 to 30 minutes in all. The broth that isn't absorbed should be thickened by the starch from the rice. You may not need all of the liquid, or you may need more broth or water.

4. Stir in the asparagus, crab, orange zest, garlic, parsley, pepper, and the remaining 1 tablespoon butter. Cook until heated through.

DIRTY RICE WITH SHRIMP

Typically, in this popular Acadian classic, it's chopped chicken livers and ground meat that make rice look "dirty." For our special version, we've left out the livers and added shrimp but kept the rest of the usual lineup—onion, celery, bell pepper, and garlic.

WINE RECOMMENDATION
These assertive and varied flavors require a simple and fruity red wine, such as Beaujolais. This wine is at its best in its frisky youth; buy the most recent vintage you can find. Luckily, both 1995 and 1996 were terrific years, so your choices are plentiful.

SERVES 4

   2 tablespoons cooking oil

½ pound ground pork

   1 onion, chopped

   2 ribs celery, diced

   1 green bell pepper, diced

   1 clove garlic, minced

¼ teaspoon cayenne

½ teaspoon paprika

½ teaspoon dried oregano

   1 bay leaf

1¾ teaspoons salt

¼ teaspoon fresh-ground black pepper

1½ cups long-grain rice

   3 cups canned low-sodium chicken broth or homemade stock

   1 pound medium shrimp, shelled and halved

   2 scallions including green tops, chopped

1. In a large saucepan, heat 1 tablespoon of the oil over moderate heat. Add the pork and cook until the meat is no longer pink, about 2 minutes.

2. Reduce the heat to moderately low and add the remaining tablespoon oil to the pan. Add the onion, celery, bell pepper, and garlic. Cover and cook, stirring occasionally, until the vegetables start to soften, about 5 minutes. Stir in the cayenne, paprika, oregano, bay leaf, salt, black pepper, and rice. Cook for 1 minute, stirring. Add the broth. Bring to a boil, reduce the heat, and simmer, covered, for 15 minutes.

3. Raise the heat to moderate and stir in the shrimp. Cover and cook for 2 minutes. Remove the pan from the heat and let stand, covered, until the rice and shrimp are just done, about 5 minutes longer. Remove the bay leaf. Stir in the scallions.

SALMON WITH THAI RICE SALAD

Rich broiled salmon rests atop a lean vegetable-and-rice salad to make a beautifully balanced meal. The Asian dressing includes big-impact flavors—fish sauce, lime juice, and cayenne—but very little oil.

WINE RECOMMENDATION
Rieslings are among the most versatile of white wines and one of the few that work well with salads. With this Thai-inspired dish, try a simple kabinett from Germany's Mosel region.

SERVES 4

1½   cups long-grain rice

3   tablespoons lime juice (from about 2 limes)

3   tablespoons Asian fish sauce (nam pla or nuoc mam)*

2   tablespoons cooking oil

3½   teaspoons sugar

Pinch cayenne

1   cucumber, peeled, halved lengthwise, seeded, and cut into ¼-inch dice

3   carrots, grated

4   scallions including green tops, chopped

6   tablespoons chopped cilantro or fresh parsley

2   pounds skinless center-cut salmon fillet, cut into 4 pieces

¼   teaspoon salt

¼   teaspoon fresh-ground black pepper

*Available at Asian markets and many supermarkets

1. Stir the rice into a medium pot of boiling, salted water and cook until just done, about 10 minutes. Drain. Rinse with cold water and drain thoroughly.

2. In a large glass or stainless-steel bowl, combine the lime juice, fish sauce, 1 tablespoon of the oil, the sugar, and cayenne. Let sit for about 5 minutes. Stir in the rice, cucumber, carrots, scallions, and cilantro.

3. Heat the broiler. Oil a broiler pan or baking sheet. Coat the salmon with the remaining 1 tablespoon oil and sprinkle with the salt and pepper. Put the salmon on the pan. Broil until just barely done (the fish should still be translucent in the center), about 5 minutes for a 1-inch-thick fillet. Put the rice salad on plates and top with the salmon.

INDONESIAN COCONUT RICE WITH CHICKEN AND ZUCCHINI

Luscious is the word for this Indonesian version of chicken and rice. Coconut milk spiced with cumin and coriander cooks into the rice and sauces the whole dish.

WINE RECOMMENDATION

A flamboyant gewürztraminer is in its element with spices such as coriander and cumin. Look to one from Alsace for full body, a delicate rose-petal aroma, and spicy apricot flavor.

SERVES 4

2 tablespoons cooking oil

8 chicken thighs

2 teaspoons salt

½ teaspoon fresh-ground black pepper

1 large onion, cut into thin slices

2 cloves garlic, minced

1½ teaspoons ground coriander

1½ teaspoons ground cumin

1½ cups long-grain rice

1⅔ cups unsweetened coconut milk (one 13-ounce can)

1¾ cups water

1 pound zucchini, cut into ¼-inch dice

1 tablespoon lemon juice

⅓ cup chopped cilantro (optional)

1. In a large deep frying pan or Dutch oven, heat the cooking oil over moderately high heat. Sprinkle the chicken with ½ teaspoon of the salt and ¼ teaspoon of the pepper. Put the chicken in the pan and brown well on both sides, about 8 minutes in all. Remove. Pour off all but 1 tablespoon of the fat. Reduce the heat to moderately low.

2. Add the onion and cook, stirring occasionally, until soft, about 5 minutes. Add the garlic and cook 1 minute longer. Stir in the coriander, cumin, rice, and the remaining 1½ teaspoons salt and ¼ teaspoon pepper. Cook, stirring, for 1 minute.

3. Stir in the coconut milk and the water. Add the chicken and bring to a simmer. Cover and cook over low heat, stirring the rice two or three times, until the rice and chicken are almost done, about 20 minutes. Stir in the zucchini, cover, and cook until done, about 7 minutes longer. Stir the lemon juice and cilantro into the rice.

THAI ONE-POT

Ground pork, rice, bell peppers, and shiitake mushrooms are cooked in a single pan and flavored with soy sauce, lime juice, and cayenne. Quick, delicious, and easy to clean up after—what more could you want in a dish?

WINE RECOMMENDATION
The zesty acidity and vivid citrus flavor of a dry riesling will partner the lime juice and cilantro beautifully. Pick one from Alsace, but stick with a lean, crisp style such as that from the venerable producer F. E. Trimbach.

SERVES 4

  1 tablespoon cooking oil

  1 green bell pepper, cut into ¼-inch strips

  1 red bell pepper, cut into ¼-inch strips

  ¼ pound shiitake mushrooms, stems removed, caps cut into ¼-inch slices

  1 teaspoon salt

  1¼ pounds lean ground pork

  ¾ cup short-grain rice

  2½ cups canned low-sodium chicken broth or homemade stock

  3 tablespoons soy sauce

  ¼ teaspoon cayenne

  4 scallions including green tops, chopped

  10 radishes, cut into thin slices

  5 tablespoons chopped cilantro or fresh parsley

  2 tablespoons lime juice (from about 1 lime)

1. In a large nonstick frying pan, heat the oil over moderately high heat. Add the bell peppers, shiitakes, and ¼ teaspoon of the salt and cook, stirring occasionally, until beginning to brown, about 5 minutes. Remove.

2. Add the pork to the pan and cook, stirring, until it is no longer pink, about 3 minutes. Spoon off the fat from the pan. Stir in the bell peppers and shiitakes, the rice, broth, soy sauce, the remaining ¾ teaspoon salt, and the cayenne. Bring to a simmer. Cover. Reduce the heat to low and simmer, without removing the lid, until the rice is just done, about 20 minutes.

3. Remove the pot from the heat and let stand, covered, for 10 minutes. Stir in the scallions, radishes, cilantro, and lime juice.

EVEN QUICKER

The radishes that are stirred in at the last minute add a pleasant crunch. For a similar effect without the slicing time, substitute one cup of bean sprouts.

RICE WITH MOZZARELLA, PROSCIUTTO, AND PEAS

Arborio rice, familiar from risotto, is simply boiled here and then tossed with peas, fresh mozzarella, Parmesan, and prosciutto. As soon as the mozzarella hits the heat, it melts to a delicate net that holds all the ingredients together.

WINE RECOMMENDATION
The traditional style of Italian white wines is crisp, clean, light-bodied, and fairly neutral in flavor—an ideal combination that won't overpower this dish. Soave, Frascati, and Orvieto will all work well, but a Vernaccia di San Gimignano, with its slightly fuller body and almond aroma, will be best of all.

SERVES 4

1½   cups arborio rice

½   cup frozen petite peas

6   ounces fresh mozzarella, grated (about 1½ cups)

½   cup grated Parmesan

3   tablespoons butter

3   ounces sliced prosciutto, cut into thin strips

½   teaspoon salt

3   tablespoons chopped fresh parsley

1.   Stir the rice into a medium pot of boiling, salted water and cook until almost done, about 15 minutes. Stir in the peas. Cook until the peas and rice are just done, about 2 minutes longer. Drain.

2.   Put the rice and peas back in the hot pot. Stir in the mozzarella, Parmesan, butter, prosciutto, salt, and parsley. Serve immediately.

VARIATIONS

■ Vary the herb here if you have access to a good fresh one. Chopped **mint**, **chervil**, **sage**, or **fennel** leaves would all be excellent.

■ For a sharper-tasting dish, substitute ½ cup grated **Pecorino Romano** for the grated Parmesan, or use a combination of the two.

FRESH MOZZARELLA

Fresh mozzarella is a soft, mild white cheese that combines well with strong-flavored ingredients. The cheese, which is formed into a ball and usually packed floating in water in a plastic tub, is available both salted and unsalted. We find the unsalted variety too bland; a light salting brings out the cheese's elusive fresh-milk flavor.

BEEF FRIED RICE

Stir-fry the sirloin, watercress, and egg while the rice cooks, so that you'll be ready to assemble the dish at the last moment. Soy sauce and a drizzling of sesame oil flavor the combination perfectly. If you prefer, use strips of pork tenderloin instead of beef.

WINE RECOMMENDATION
A California merlot, with its plum flavor and undercurrents of chocolate and herbs, makes a rich accompaniment to the beefy rice. As always with California wines, try to find one that is lightly oaked; a heavy oak taste tends to overwhelm food.

SERVES 4

¾ pound sirloin steak, cut into ½-inch cubes

3 tablespoons plus 1 teaspoon soy sauce

2 teaspoons Asian sesame oil, plus a few drops
Dried red-pepper flakes

1½ cups long-grain rice

1 bunch watercress (about 5 ounces), tough stems removed

1 egg, beaten to mix

3 tablespoons cooking oil

2 scallions including green tops, chopped

1. In a medium bowl, combine the sirloin with 1 tablespoon of the soy sauce, 1 teaspoon of the sesame oil, and a pinch of red-pepper flakes. Bring a medium pot of salted water to a boil. Stir in the rice and boil until just done, about 10 minutes. Drain the rice and return it to the pot.

2. Meanwhile, heat a large nonstick frying pan over moderately high heat. Put the beef mixture in the pan and cook, stirring occasionally, until browned and just cooked, 1 to 2 minutes. Remove. Put the watercress and the teaspoon of soy sauce in the pan and cook until the watercress is just wilted, about 30 seconds. Remove.

3. Reduce the heat to moderate. Put a few drops of sesame oil in the frying pan. Add the egg to the pan and cook until just done, about 30 seconds. Remove from the pan and cut into thin strips.

4. Heat the cooking oil in the pan over moderately high heat. Add the scallions and ⅛ teaspoon red-pepper flakes and cook, stirring, for 1 minute. Add the cooked rice to the pan and heat, stirring, for 3 minutes. Add the remaining 2 tablespoons soy sauce, the beef, watercress, and egg. Heat, stirring, 1 to 2 minutes longer. Drizzle the remaining teaspoon of sesame oil over the top.

LAMB BIRYANI

Our quick version of this usually labor-intensive Indian rice dish is intricately spiced and irresistibly delicious. Don't let the long ingredient list put you off; almost everything is a pantry staple. Indian cooks leave the whole cloves and pieces of cinnamon in when serving, but of course they don't eat them. Fish these spices out before serving if you prefer.

WINE RECOMMENDATION
The spices here immediately indicate a zinfandel from Napa or Sonoma, classic examples of which are redolent of the very same spices. The full body of these wines will match the intensity of the biryani nicely.

SERVES 4

½   cup plain yogurt
2   cloves garlic, minced
⅛   teaspoon cayenne
½   teaspoon ground cumin
¼   teaspoon fresh-ground black pepper
1¾   teaspoons salt
1   pound boneless lamb, cut into ½-inch cubes
3   tablespoons butter
1   onion, cut into thin slices
¼   teaspoon ground cardamom or ground coriander
¼   teaspoon turmeric
5   cloves
1   cinnamon stick, broken in half
1½   cups long-grain rice, preferably basmati
2¾   cups water
⅓   cup raisins
⅓   cup chopped cashews

1. In a medium bowl, combine the yogurt with the garlic, cayenne, cumin, black pepper, and ½ teaspoon of the salt. Stir in the lamb.

2. In a large saucepan, melt the butter over moderate heat. Add the onion and cook until starting to soften, about 3 minutes. Stir in the cardamom, turmeric, cloves, cinnamon, rice, and the remaining 1¼ teaspoons salt. Cook, stirring, for 1 minute.

3. Add the lamb mixture to the pan. Stir in the water and raisins. Bring to a simmer. Cover and simmer until the rice and lamb are almost done, about 20 minutes. Remove from the heat. Let stand, covered, until the rice and lamb are just done, about 5 minutes. Stir in the cashews.

VARIATION

Other nuts, such as **almonds** or **pistachios**, can easily stand in for the cashews.

55

SHRIMP WITH MINTY COUSCOUS SALAD

Tiny frozen peas are a time-saver here, since they require no cooking, just thawing. They also happen to taste better than most of the fresh peas available. The tomato, though, needs to be fresh and vine ripened. If you can't get a good one, omit it.

WINE RECOMMENDATION
Mint is one of those ingredients that can be tricky to pair with wine, but sauvignon blanc handles it well. The wine also marries beautifully with shrimp and peas. Choose one from either Alto Adige or Friuli, both in northeastern Italy.

SERVES 4

1½   cups canned low-sodium chicken broth or homemade stock

1¾   teaspoons salt

1   cup plus 2 tablespoons couscous

1   large tomato, cut into small dice

1   cup frozen petite peas, thawed

½   cup chopped fresh mint

5   tablespoons olive oil

2   tablespoons lemon juice

Fresh-ground black pepper

1   pound large shrimp, shelled

1. In a medium saucepan, bring the broth and 1 teaspoon of the salt to a boil. Stir in the couscous. Cover, remove from the heat, and let stand 5 minutes. Transfer to a large bowl and let cool. Add the tomato, peas, mint, 4 tablespoons of the oil, the lemon juice, ½ teaspoon of the salt, and ¼ teaspoon pepper to the couscous.

2. In a large nonstick frying pan, heat the remaining 1 tablespoon oil over moderately high heat. Add the shrimp, the remaining ¼ teaspoon salt, and ⅛ teaspoon pepper. Cook turning, until just done, about 3 minutes in all. Serve the couscous salad topped with the shrimp.

VARIATION

Replace the shrimp with **sea scallops**. Cook the scallops in the same way and for about the same length of time, until they just turn opaque.

SWORDFISH WITH VEGETABLE COUSCOUS AND TOMATO VINAIGRETTE

A fluffy mound of couscous, studded with diced fennel and summer squash, makes a lovely bed for a succulent seared swordfish steak. Topping it off is a vinaigrette that's chunky with fresh plum tomatoes. If you like, you can grill or broil the swordfish steaks instead of sautéing them.

WINE RECOMMENDATION
Red wine with fish? When it's a fatty fish such as swordfish and the wine is pinot noir, the combination can't be beat. To see just how well it works, try an Oregon pinot noir, brimming with fresh red berries and subtle earth tones.

SERVES 4

1/2 pound plum tomatoes (about 4)

1 1/2 teaspoons wine vinegar

3 tablespoons olive oil

1/2 teaspoon dried oregano
Fresh-ground black pepper

1 3/4 teaspoons salt

2 scallions including green tops, chopped

1 fennel bulb, cut into 1/4-inch dice

1 summer squash, cut into 1/4-inch dice

2 1/2 cups canned low-sodium chicken broth or homemade stock

1 1/3 cups couscous

4 swordfish steaks (about 2 pounds in all)

1. In a blender, combine the tomatoes with the vinegar, 1 tablespoon of the oil, 1/4 teaspoon of the oregano, 1/4 teaspoon pepper, and 1/2 teaspoon salt. Pulse to combine, leaving small chunks of chopped tomato. Don't puree or the vinaigrette will be too frothy.

2. In a large saucepan, heat 1 tablespoon of the oil over moderate heat. Add the scallions and fennel and cook, stirring, for 2 minutes. Stir in the squash, the remaining 1/4 teaspoon oregano, and 1/4 teaspoon pepper. Cover and cook for 4 minutes. Add the broth and bring to a simmer. Stir in 1 teaspoon of the salt and the couscous. Cover. Remove the pot from the heat and let the couscous stand for 5 minutes. Fluff with a fork.

3. Meanwhile, in a large nonstick frying pan, heat the remaining 1 tablespoon oil over moderately high heat. Sprinkle the swordfish with the remaining 1/4 teaspoon salt and 1/8 teaspoon of pepper. Add the fish to the pan and cook for 3 minutes. Turn and cook until golden brown and just done, 2 to 3 minutes longer for 3/4-inch-thick steaks. Serve the swordfish on the couscous and top each steak with tomato vinaigrette.

COUSCOUS WITH CHICKEN AND CHICKPEAS

Served on a mound of couscous, with plenty of steaming broth poured over the top, this hearty Moroccan-inspired stew is a flavorful combination of chicken, chickpeas, vegetables, and spices.

WINE RECOMMENDATION
Often with a complex dish it's best to serve a simple wine that won't compete with the food's flavors. Here, an exuberantly fruity Beaujolais-Villages will effectively highlight the stew.

SERVES 4

2	tablespoons cooking oil
8	chicken drumsticks
3	teaspoons salt
1/4	teaspoon fresh-ground black pepper
1	onion, cut into thin slices
1	turnip, peeled and cut into 1/2-inch cubes
2	tablespoons tomato paste
1	teaspoon paprika
1 1/2	teaspoons ground cumin
1/8	teaspoon cayenne
6	cups water
3	carrots, cut into 1/4-inch slices
1 2/3	cups drained and rinsed canned chickpeas (one 15-ounce can)
1/2	cup packed flat-leaf parsley leaves
1 1/3	cups couscous

1. In a large deep frying pan or Dutch oven, heat the oil over moderately high heat. Sprinkle the chicken with 1/2 teaspoon of the salt and the black pepper. Put the chicken in the pan and brown well, about 8 minutes in all. Remove. Pour off all but 1 tablespoon of the fat. Reduce the heat to moderately low.

2. Add the onion and turnip and cook, stirring occasionally, for 3 minutes. Stir in the tomato paste, paprika, cumin, cayenne, and 2 1/4 teaspoons of the salt. Cook, stirring, for 1 minute. Stir in 4 cups of the water and the carrots. Add the chicken and bring to a simmer. Cover and cook, stirring the mixture two or three times, until the chicken and vegetables are almost done, about 20 minutes. Stir in the chickpeas and the parsley and simmer until the chicken and vegetables are done, about 5 minutes longer.

3. Meanwhile, in a medium saucepan, bring the remaining 2 cups water to a boil. Add the remaining 1/4 teaspoon salt and the couscous. Cover. Remove the pot from the heat and let the couscous stand for 5 minutes. Fluff with a fork. Serve the stew with its broth over the couscous.

SAUSAGE AND BROCCOLI RABE WITH POLENTA

Spicy Italian sausage and broccoli rabe simmer in a flavorful tomato sauce. Served over a mound of creamy polenta, they make a ravishing, rustic Italian meal for a cold winter's night. If you like, pass grated Parmesan at the table.

WINE RECOMMENDATION
This rustic dish wants a red wine, but the the broccoli rabe's bite will combine with tannin to create an unpleasant bitterness. Opt for an Italian barbera; it has minimal tannin.

SERVES 4

1	pound broccoli rabe, tough stems removed
4	tablespoons olive oil
1⅓	pounds hot or mild Italian sausage
1	onion, chopped
2	cloves garlic, chopped
¼	cup dry white wine
1½	cups canned crushed tomatoes in thick puree (from a 14-ounce can)
1½	cups canned low-sodium chicken broth or homemade stock
½	teaspoon dried thyme
2½	teaspoons salt
¼	cup chopped flat-leaf parsley
⅛	teaspoon fresh-ground black pepper
4½	cups water
1⅓	cups coarse or medium cornmeal

1. In a large pot of boiling, salted water, cook the broccoli rabe until tender, about 2 minutes. Drain. Rinse with cold water and drain thoroughly. Cut into 2-inch lengths.

2. In a large frying pan, heat 1 tablespoon of the oil over moderately high heat. Add the sausage and cook, turning, until browned, about 10 minutes. Remove. When cool enough to handle, cut into slices.

3. Pour off all but 2 tablespoons of the fat from the pan. Reduce the heat to moderately low. Add the onion and garlic and cook, stirring occasionally, until translucent, about 5 minutes. Add the wine; bring to a simmer. Add the sausage, tomatoes, broth, thyme, and 1¼ teaspoons of the salt. Bring to a simmer. Cook, uncovered, for 15 minutes. Add the broccoli rabe, parsley, and pepper to the sauce; bring to a simmer.

4. Meanwhile, in a medium saucepan, bring the water and the remaining 1¼ teaspoons salt to a boil. Add the cornmeal in a slow stream, whisking. Whisk in the remaining 3 tablespoons oil. Reduce the heat and simmer, stirring frequently with a wooden spoon, until very thick, about 20 minutes. Serve with the sauce.

FLANK STEAK OVER CORN-KERNEL POLENTA

The brown glaze left in the pan after sautéing the steak is the base for a highly concentrated sauce. A cup of white wine and a half cup of brandy deglaze the pan and then cook down to a mere quarter cup. If you taste the sauce on its own, you may find it too strong, but drizzled over the steak, it's divine.

WINE RECOMMENDATION
Cabernet sauvignon goes well with red meat, which tames the tannic wine. One from Napa Valley is just the ticket here.

SERVES 4

5½   cups water
2¼   teaspoons salt
¾   teaspoon dried thyme
2   cups fresh (cut from about 3 ears) or frozen corn kernels
1⅓   cups coarse or medium cornmeal
2   tablespoons butter
2   tablespoons cooking oil
1½   pounds flank steak
¼   teaspoon fresh-ground black pepper
2   cloves garlic, minced
1   cup dry white wine
½   cup brandy or bourbon

1. In a medium saucepan, bring the water, 1¾ teaspoons of the salt, and ½ teaspoon of the thyme to a boil. Stir in the corn and cook until tender, 5 minutes for fresh, 1 minute for frozen. Add the cornmeal in a slow stream, whisking. Reduce the heat and simmer, stirring frequently, until very thick, about 20 minutes. Remove from the heat. Stir in the butter.

2. In a large frying pan, heat the oil over moderate heat. Sprinkle the steak with the remaining ½ teaspoon salt and the pepper. Add the meat to the pan and cook for 5 minutes. Turn and cook to your taste, about 5 minutes longer for medium rare, depending on the thickness. Remove.

3. Reduce the heat to moderately low. Add the garlic to the pan and cook, stirring, for 30 seconds. Add the remaining ¼ teaspoon thyme, the wine, and the brandy and stir to dislodge any brown bits that cling to the bottom of the pan. Boil until reduced to approximately ¼ cup, 3 to 4 minutes. Slice the steak across the grain and on the diagonal. Serve the steak over a bed of corn polenta, with the sauce drizzled over all.

CHAPTER THREE

Soups
&
Stews

TUSCAN TOMATO BREAD SOUP WITH STEAMED MUSSELS

There are many versions of bread soup; this one, based on traditional peasant fare, is as thick as a bread pudding. The soup is delicious on its own, but we think the steamed mussels with their broth make a wonderful addition.

WINE RECOMMENDATION
With such a regional dish, the wine almost has to come from Tuscany, too. Try a Rosso di Montalcino, Brunello's lighter, less costly cousin.

SERVES 4

- 6 tablespoons olive oil
- 1 onion, chopped fine
- 1 red bell pepper, chopped fine
- 6 cloves garlic, minced
- ¼ cup chopped fresh basil plus 2 tablespoons thin-sliced basil leaves
- ½ teaspoon dried oregano
- 2 cups canned crushed tomatoes in thick puree (from one 28-ounce can)
- 1¼ pounds vine-ripened tomatoes (about 4), cut into small dice
- 1 cup canned low-sodium chicken broth or homemade stock
- 2¼ teaspoons salt
   Pinch sugar
- 1 ¾-pound country loaf, crust removed, cut into 1-inch cubes (about 7 cups)
- ¼ teaspoon fresh-ground black pepper
- 2 pounds mussels, scrubbed and debearded
- ¼ cup dry white wine

1. In a large saucepan, heat 4 tablespoons of the oil over moderately low heat. Add the onion, bell pepper, garlic, chopped basil, and oregano. Cook, stirring occasionally, until the onion is golden, about 10 minutes. Add the canned and fresh tomatoes, the broth, salt, and sugar; bring to a simmer. Reduce the heat to low. Simmer, uncovered, until thick, about 30 minutes.

2. Meanwhile, heat the oven to 350°. Put the bread on a baking sheet and toast in the oven until crisp, about 25 minutes. Remove. Add the bread and the pepper to the sauce and bring to a simmer. Cook, stirring gently, until the bread absorbs all the liquid, about 5 minutes.

3. Discard any mussels that have broken shells or that don't clamp shut when tapped. Put the wine, mussels, and 1 tablespoon of the oil in a large stainless-steel saucepan. Cover and bring to a boil over high heat. Cook, shaking the pot occasionally, just until the mussels open, about 3 minutes. Discard any mussels that do not open. Mound the bread soup in shallow bowls and surround with the mussels and broth, leaving any grit in the pan. Drizzle with the remaining 1 tablespoon oil and sprinkle with the sliced basil.

SALMON-AND-CORN CHOWDER WITH LIMA BEANS

Where most chowders have milk as their base, this one uses chicken stock and pureed corn, with a little half-and-half stirred in just before serving to make it nice and creamy.

WINE RECOMMENDATION
Pinot blanc from Alsace is delicious, plentiful, and inexpensive. It will provide a lovely backdrop for the chowder's rich flavor and texture.

SERVES 4

¼ pound sliced bacon, cut crosswise into thin strips

1 onion, chopped

1¼ pounds boiling potatoes (about 3), peeled and cut into ½-inch dice

3 cups canned low-sodium chicken broth or homemade stock

1¾ teaspoons salt

2⅔ cups fresh (cut from about 4 ears) or frozen corn kernels

1 pound skinless salmon fillets, cut into 1-inch pieces

1 cup frozen baby lima beans, thawed

⅛ teaspoon fresh-ground black pepper

¾ cup half-and-half

2 tablespoons chopped chives or scallion tops

1. In a large pot, cook the bacon until crisp. Remove with a slotted spoon and drain on paper towels. Pour off all but 1 tablespoon of fat from the pot. Add the onion and cook over moderately low heat, stirring occasionally, until translucent, about 5 minutes.

2. Add the potatoes, broth, bacon, and ½ teaspoon of the salt to the pot and simmer, covered, for 10 minutes. Put the corn kernels in a food processor and pulse six to eight times to chop. Add the corn to the pot and cook, covered, until the potatoes and corn are just done, about 5 minutes longer.

3. Add the salmon, lima beans, the remaining 1¼ teaspoons salt, and the pepper. Bring just back to a simmer; the fish should be just cooked through. Stir in the half-and-half and serve the chowder topped with the chives.

VARIATION

If you're not a lima-bean fan, substitute another vegetable, such as **petite peas**.

71

TORTILLA SOUP

From south of the border comes this spicy and hearty soup ladled over crisp tortilla strips and grated cheddar. The soup is chunky with chicken and avocado, but it's the tortillas that give it a slight thickness and a special flavor.

WINE RECOMMENDATION
A Rioja Reserva, with its complex combination of spicy, earthy, and fruity flavors, will echo the taste of the soup beautifully.

SERVES 4

6 tablespoons cooking oil

8 6-inch corn tortillas, halved and cut crosswise into ¼-inch strips

1 onion, chopped

4 large cloves garlic, smashed

1 tablespoon paprika

2 teaspoons ground cumin

1 teaspoon ground coriander

1 teaspoon chili powder

¼ teaspoon cayenne

1½ quarts canned low-sodium chicken broth or homemade stock

3 cups canned crushed tomatoes in thick puree (one 28-ounce can)

2 bay leaves

2½ teaspoons salt

¼ cup lightly-packed cilantro leaves plus 3 tablespoons chopped cilantro (optional)

1¾ pounds boneless, skinless chicken breasts, cut into ¾-inch pieces

1 avocado, cut into ½-inch dice

¼ pound cheddar, grated

Lime wedges, for serving

1. In a large heavy pot, heat the oil over moderately high heat. Add half the tortilla strips and cook, stirring, until pale golden, about 1 minute. Remove with a slotted spoon and drain on paper towels. Repeat with the remaining tortilla strips.

2. Reduce the heat to moderately low. Add the onion, garlic, and spices; cook, stirring, for 5 minutes. Add the broth, tomatoes, bay leaves, salt, cilantro leaves, if using, and one-third of the tortilla strips. Bring to a simmer. Cook, uncovered, for 30 minutes; remove the bay leaves.

3. In a blender, puree the soup in batches; pour it back into the pot. Add the chicken, bring the soup back to a simmer, and cook until just done, about 1 minute. Stir in the avocado.

4. To serve, put the remaining tortilla strips in bowls, top with the cheese, and pour in the soup. Sprinkle with the chopped cilantro, if using, and serve with the lime wedges.

ASIAN CHICKEN NOODLE SOUP

Spaghettini is a good stand-in for Asian noodles, but if you can find rice noodles, by all means use them here. Serve the soup in deep bowls with chopsticks or forks as well as spoons. Eat the noodles first and then drink the soup in the Asian manner. Or, to use a spoon only and eat everything together, break the pasta into small pieces before cooking.

WINE RECOMMENDATION
The piquant Asian juxtaposition of fiery and savory elements demands the cooling influence of an off-dry German riesling. Try a luscious spätlese from the Pfalz.

SERVES 4

1 tablespoon cooking oil

1 tablespoon Asian sesame oil

1 onion, chopped

2 ribs celery, cut into ¼-inch slices

4 cloves garlic, smashed

1 1-inch piece fresh ginger, cut into thin slices

2 tablespoons chili powder

⅛ teaspoon dried red-pepper flakes

1½ quarts canned low-sodium chicken broth or homemade stock

1 cup canned crushed tomatoes in thick puree

1½ pounds boneless, skinless chicken thighs

3 tablespoons Asian fish sauce (nam pla or nuoc mam)*

1 cup cilantro leaves plus ¼ cup chopped cilantro (optional)

1¾ teaspoons salt

½ pound spaghettini

½ head bok choy (about 1 pound), cut crosswise into ¼-inch slices

¼ cup lime juice (from about 2 limes)

*Available at Asian markets and many supermarkets

1. In a large heavy pot, heat both oils over moderate heat. Add the onion, celery, garlic, ginger, chili powder, and red-pepper flakes. Cook, stirring occasionally, for 5 minutes.

2. Add the broth, tomatoes, chicken, fish sauce, cilantro leaves, if using, and the salt and bring to a simmer. Reduce the heat and simmer, covered, until the chicken is just done, about 15 minutes. Remove the chicken; when it is cool enough to handle, cut it into bite-size pieces. Continue cooking the soup for 15 minutes longer.

3. Meanwhile, in a large pot of boiling, salted water, cook the spaghettini until just done, about 9 minutes. Drain and add the pasta and the chicken to the soup.

4. Add the bok choy; bring back to a simmer. Cook until just done, about 1 minute. Stir in the lime juice and chopped cilantro, if using.

CHICKEN AND SMOKED-SAUSAGE GUMBO

The flavor of browned roux is essential to the traditional taste of Louisiana gumbo. So don't worry if the flour mixture looks like peanut butter by the time the vegetables have softened. That's just as it should be.

WINE RECOMMENDATION
No region of the wine world is producing more exciting wine bargains than the Languedoc-Roussillon in southern France. Try any one of their sturdy reds with this hearty gumbo.

SERVES 4

3 tablespoons cooking oil

3 tablespoons flour

1 onion, chopped

2 ribs celery, chopped

1 green bell pepper, chopped

1 10-ounce package frozen sliced okra

1 bay leaf

1½ teaspoons dried thyme

1 teaspoon dried oregano

2 teaspoons salt

¼ teaspoon fresh-ground black pepper

¼ teaspoon cayenne

1¾ cups canned crushed tomatoes in thick puree (one 15-ounce can)

1 quart canned low-sodium chicken broth or homemade stock

½ pound smoked sausage, halved lengthwise and cut crosswise into ¼-inch slices

1 pound boneless, skinless chicken breasts, cut into ¾-inch pieces

¾ cup long-grain rice

1. In a large stainless-steel pot, heat the oil over moderate heat. Whisk in the flour and cook, whisking, until starting to brown, about 4 minutes. Reduce the heat to moderately low. Stir in the onion, celery, and bell pepper and cook until starting to soften, about 7 minutes. Add the okra, bay leaf, thyme, oregano, salt, black pepper, cayenne, and tomatoes. Cover and cook for 5 minutes.

2. Stir in the broth and the smoked sausage. Bring to a boil. Reduce the heat and simmer for 15 minutes. Add the chicken and cook until just done, 4 to 5 minutes longer. Remove the bay leaf.

3. Meanwhile, bring a medium pot of salted water to a boil. Stir in the rice and boil until just done, 10 to 12 minutes. Drain. Put a mound of rice in the center of each bowl. Ladle the gumbo around the rice.

TURKEY AND SWEET-POTATO SOUP

Turkey, sweet potatoes, sage—it's Thanksgiving in a bowl! Half of the sweet-potato mixture is pureed, thickening the soup every so slightly and coloring it a pretty pale orange.

WINE RECOMMENDATION
Sweet wines are said not to work at the table, but when the dish contains sweet elements, the wine often should, too. A cool glass of succulent auslese riesling from the Rheingau will prove the point quite elegantly.

SERVES 4

2 tablespoons butter

1 onion, cut into thin slices

1½ teaspoons dried sage

1 pound sweet potatoes, peeled and cut into ½-inch cubes

1½ quarts canned low-sodium chicken broth or homemade stock

2 teaspoons salt

¼ pound green beans, cut into ¼-inch pieces

¼ teaspoon fresh-ground black pepper

1 pound turkey cutlets, cut into approximately 1½-by-½-inch strips

1. In a large pot, melt the butter over moderately low heat. Add the onion and sage and cook, stirring occasionally, until the onion is translucent, about 5 minutes.

2. Add the sweet potatoes, broth, and 1 teaspoon of the salt. Bring to a boil. Reduce the heat and simmer until the sweet potatoes are tender, about 10 minutes.

3. Transfer half the soup to a food processor or blender and puree. Return the pureed soup to the pot and add the green beans, the remaining teaspoon salt, and the pepper. Simmer until the beans are just tender, about 8 minutes.

4. Stir in the strips of turkey. Cook until the turkey is just done, about 1½ minutes.

TURKEY OPTIONS

If you like, buy a three-quarter-pound piece of cooked turkey breast from the deli to use instead of the turkey cutlets. Cut the turkey into half-inch cubes and heat it in the soup briefly. Another option is to use leftover cooked turkey or chicken. About two cups of cubed leftovers should do it.

TURKEY AND BLACK-BEAN SOUP

Ribbons of bright green spinach float in a rich-tasting broth that's chock-full of turkey, black beans, and bacon. The soup may remind you of chili, and in fact it's flavored with chili powder, along with cocoa, oregano, and Tabasco sauce.

WINE RECOMMENDATION
You need a lusty red wine with plenty of spiciness and fruit flavor to stand up to this powerful soup. That describes zinfandel to a T, so try one here.

SERVES 4

¼ pound sliced bacon, cut crosswise into ¼-inch strips

1 onion, chopped

1 tablespoon chili powder

½ teaspoon unsweetened cocoa powder

¼ teaspoon Tabasco sauce

2 teaspoons dried oregano

2 teaspoons salt

¼ teaspoon fresh-ground black pepper

1¾ cups canned crushed tomatoes in thick puree (one 15-ounce can)

1 quart canned low-sodium chicken broth or homemade stock

1⅔ cups drained and rinsed canned black beans (one 15-ounce can)

1 1-pound piece cooked deli turkey, cut into ½-by-½-by-¼-inch slices

10 ounces spinach, stems removed, leaves washed and cut crosswise into 1-inch strips

1. In a large stainless-steel pot, cook the bacon until crisp. Remove with a slotted spoon and drain on paper towels. Pour off all but 1 tablespoon of fat from the pot.

2. Reduce the heat to moderately low. Add the onion to the pot and cook, stirring, until translucent, about 5 minutes. Stir in the chili powder, cocoa, Tabasco sauce, oregano, salt, pepper, tomatoes, and broth. Bring to a boil. Reduce the heat and simmer for 15 minutes.

3. Add the black beans and turkey to the pot. Simmer for 5 minutes. Stir in the spinach and the bacon. Cook until the spinach just wilts, about 1 minute.

VARIATIONS

■ Use **smoked turkey** in place of plain.

■ Substitute 1⅔ cups drained and rinsed **kidney**, **pinto**, or **cannellini** beans for the black beans.

GINGERED CABBAGE SOUP WITH PORK AND POTATOES

A sprightly ginger broth transforms typical cabbage, pork, and potato soup into a meal that's light-tasting and satisfying at the same time. The shot of lemon juice added at the end intensifies the flavors.

WINE RECOMMENDATION
Tokay Pinot Gris is full and very rich, with gentle acidity and a nutty flavor. You'll be surprised how well it performs here.

SERVES 4

2 tablespoons butter

1 onion, chopped

1 tablespoon minced fresh ginger, plus one 2-inch piece, peeled, halved lengthwise, and smashed

¾ pound green cabbage (about ¼ head), shredded (about 3 cups)

1½ quarts canned low-sodium chicken broth or homemade stock

1 pound boiling potatoes (about 3), peeled and cut into ½-inch cubes

2 teaspoons salt

1 pound pork tenderloin, cut into approximately 1½-inch-long-by-¼-inch-wide strips

2 teaspoons lemon juice

¼ cup chopped fresh parsley

1. In a large pot, melt the butter over moderately low heat. Add the onion and cook, stirring occasionally, until starting to soften, about 3 minutes. Stir in the minced ginger and the cabbage and cook for 1 minute longer.

2. Add the broth, potatoes, smashed ginger, and 1 teaspoon of the salt. Bring to a boil. Reduce the heat and simmer until the potatoes are tender, about 10 minutes.

3. Stir in the pork and the remaining 1 teaspoon salt. Cook until the pork is just done, about 3 minutes. Stir in the lemon juice and parsley. Remove the pieces of smashed ginger before serving.

FRESH GINGER

You'll want to use really fresh ginger here; it's integral to the flavoring of the soup. Look for a piece that has taut skin and is firm to the touch. After the ginger is peeled (the easiest way is to scrape the peel off with a spoon), its color should be pale yellow. If the ginger is blueish green instead, chances are the piece is old and won't have the vibrant flavor you're looking for.

SHELLFISH STEW WITH CHORIZO AND ROUILLE

Rouille, the zesty garlic and red-pepper sauce served with bouillabaisse, is stirred into this shrimp-and-scallop dish at the last minute, and it's also spread on the croûtes that top it.

WINE RECOMMENDATION

The rich, earthy rosés of Provence go particularly well with shellfish stews. Look for a wine from the commune of Bandol, especially from the great Domaines Ott.

SERVES 4

1½ teaspoons olive oil

¾ pound cured chorizo or other spicy hard sausage such as pepperoni, casings removed and sausage cut into ¼-inch slices

1 onion, chopped

½ cup dry white wine

10 cloves garlic, 4 minced, 6 smashed

3 cups bottled clam juice

1½ cups canned crushed tomatoes in thick puree (one 15-ounce can)

½ teaspoon dried thyme

1½ teaspoons salt

1 baguette

½ cup mayonnaise

⅓ cup drained bottled roasted red peppers

¼ teaspoon cayenne

¾ pound large shrimp, shelled

¾ pound sea scallops, cut in half if very large

¼ teaspoon fresh-ground black pepper

1. In a large pot, heat the oil over moderately high heat. Add the chorizo and cook, stirring frequently, until browned, about 10 minutes. Remove. Pour off all but 1 tablespoon fat.

2. Reduce the heat to moderately low. Add the onion and cook, stirring occasionally, until translucent, about 5 minutes. Add the wine and the minced garlic, bring to a simmer, and cook until reduced to about ¼ cup, about 3 minutes. Add the cooked chorizo, the clam juice, tomatoes, thyme, and 1 teaspoon of the salt. Cover, bring to a simmer, and let simmer for 20 minutes.

3. Meanwhile, cut a 3-inch piece from the baguette and remove the crust. Hold this bread under running water to soften; squeeze to remove the water. Put this bread in a food processor. Add the mayonnaise, red peppers, cayenne, and the remaining garlic and ½ teaspoon salt and puree.

4. Light the broiler. Cut the remaining baguette into ¼-inch slices and broil the bread on both sides until golden, about 3 minutes.

5. Add the shellfish to the stew; bring to a simmer, by which time they should be just done. Stir in ½ cup of the *rouille* and the black pepper. Serve with the remaining *rouille* and the croûtes.

PORK PAPRIKASH

Cubes of pork tenderloin are browned and then stewed in broth flavored with paprika, onion, and peppers. The traditional dose of sour cream thickens the sauce. To be even more authentic, brown the pork and onions in bacon fat, as the Hungarians do.

WINE RECOMMENDATION
Stay with Hungary and serve the fearsomely named *bull's blood*, Egri Bikavér. It's actually a soft, spicy, fruity red that is just perfect with this traditional stew.

SERVES 4

3 tablespoons cooking oil or bacon fat

1½ pounds pork tenderloin, cut into 1½-inch cubes

1 tablespoon flour

1¾ teaspoons salt

½ teaspoon fresh-ground black pepper

1 onion, cut into thin slices

2 large green bell peppers, cut into thin strips

4 teaspoons paprika

1½ cups canned low-sodium chicken broth or homemade stock

¾ cup sour cream

¾ pound egg noodles

1. In a large pot, heat 1 tablespoon of the oil over moderately high heat. Toss the pork with the flour, ½ teaspoon of the salt, and ¼ teaspoon of the black pepper. Add about half the pork to the pot and brown for about 3 minutes.

Remove. Repeat with the remaining pork and an additional tablespoon oil. Remove.

2. Reduce the heat to moderately low and add the remaining tablespoon oil to the pan. Add the onion and bell peppers. Cook, covered, stirring occasionally, for 7 minutes. Stir in the remaining 1¼ teaspoons salt, ¼ teaspoon black pepper, and the paprika. Cook, stirring, for 30 seconds. Add the pork with any accumulated juices and the broth. Bring to a boil, reduce the heat, and simmer, partially covered, until the pork is just done, 10 to 15 minutes. Reduce the heat to very low and whisk in the sour cream.

3. Meanwhile, in a large pot of boiling, salted water, cook the egg noodles until just done, about 7 minutes. Drain. Remove ½ cup of the sauce from the stew and toss with the noodles. Serve the stew over the noodles.

BEEF KEEMA

Although this ground-meat curry is often made with lamb, we've found that the distinctive combination of spices tastes just as good with beef. Serve the thick, chili-like *keema* with warm naan (Indian flatbread), if available, or pita.

WINE RECOMMENDATION
Whenever there are a lot of elements in a dish, it is best to keep the wine simple. Here, an uncomplicated but fruity Beaujolais will be charming.

SERVES 4

  2   tablespoons cooking oil
  1   large onion, chopped
  3   cloves garlic, minced
  1   tablespoon chopped fresh ginger
1½   pounds ground beef
2½   teaspoons ground coriander
2½   teaspoons ground cumin
  ¼   teaspoon fresh-ground black pepper
  ½   teaspoon turmeric
  ⅛   teaspoon cinnamon
1½   teaspoons salt
  1   pound boiling potatoes, peeled and cut
       into ½-inch pieces
  1   cup plain yogurt
  ¾   cup whole milk
  ¾   cup frozen petite peas
1½   teaspoons lemon juice
  ½   cup chopped cilantro

1. In a large deep frying pan, heat the oil over moderate heat. Add the onion and cook until starting to soften, about 3 minutes. Stir in the garlic and ginger and cook 1 minute longer. Add the beef and cook until no longer pink, about 3 minutes. Drain off any fat.

2. Add the coriander, cumin, pepper, turmeric, cinnamon, and 1 teaspoon of the salt to the pan. Cook, stirring, for 1 minute. Stir in the potatoes, yogurt, and milk. Bring just to a boil. Cover the pan. Reduce the heat and simmer for 20 minutes. Uncover the pan and simmer for 5 minutes longer.

3. Stir in the peas and the remaining ½ teaspoon salt. Simmer until the peas are just done, about 2 minutes. Stir in the lemon juice and the cilantro.

CHAPTER FOUR

From the Oven or Grill

ROASTED SALMON, BEETS, AND POTATOES WITH HORSERADISH CREAM

Beets and potatoes roast alongside each other in the same pan. Wait until they're cooked to toss them together, though, or you'll end up with bright-pink potatoes. A fillet of salmon roasts at the same oven temperature, and a drizzle of creamy horseradish sauce tops them all.

WINE RECOMMENDATION
In the Pacific Northwest, where they really know their seafood, pinot noir is the wine of choice with salmon. It should be yours, too. Try a fruity example from Oregon or California.

SERVES 4

1½ pounds beets, peeled and cut into ½-inch dice

2 tablespoons cooking oil

1 teaspoon salt

½ teaspoon dried dill

Fresh-ground black pepper

1½ pounds baking potatoes (about 3), peeled and cut into ½-inch dice

1½ pounds skinless salmon fillets, about 1-inch thick, cut into 4 pieces

½ cup heavy cream

2 tablespoons drained bottled horseradish

1. Heat the oven to 450°. In a large roasting pan, toss the beets with 1 tablespoon of the oil, ¼ teaspoon of the salt, ¼ teaspoon of the dill, and ⅛ teaspoon pepper. Cook in the upper third of the oven, stirring once, for 20 minutes.

2. Remove the pan from the oven and push the beets to one side. Add the potatoes to the pan, next to the beets, and toss them with the remaining 1 tablespoon oil and ¼ teaspoon of the salt. Return the pan to the oven and cook for 10 minutes. Stir the potatoes and beets, keeping them separate; return the pan to the oven.

3. Meanwhile, oil a baking sheet. Put the salmon on the baking sheet and sprinkle with ¼ teaspoon of the salt, the remaining ¼ teaspoon dill, and ⅛ teaspoon pepper. Put the pan in the oven with the vegetables (after you stir them at the end of Step 2). Cook until just done, about 10 minutes for 1-inch fillets.

4. Meanwhile, in a small saucepan, bring the cream just to a simmer. Remove from the heat and whisk in the horseradish, the remaining ¼ teaspoon salt, and a pinch of pepper.

5. Stir the beets and the potatoes together. Serve the vegetables topped with the salmon and the horseradish sauce.

ROASTED CHICKEN, NEW POTATOES, AND ASPARAGUS

The chicken, potatoes, and asparagus all roast in the oven, though for different lengths of time. You'll need to open the oven door several times; close it again quickly so that the temperature doesn't drop precipitously.

WINE RECOMMENDATION
Asparagus can make wines taste sweet, but a New Zealand sauvignon blanc will meet the challenge with high acidity and intense fruitiness. The wine has its own hints of asparagus that will echo the vegetable here.

SERVES 4

1½ pounds new potatoes, halved, or boiling potatoes, cut into ¾-inch pieces

10 cloves garlic

3½ tablespoons cooking oil
    Salt

4 bone-in chicken breasts (about 2¼ pounds in all)

1 tablespoon lemon juice
   Fresh-ground black pepper

1 tablespoon butter, cut into 4 pieces

1 pound asparagus, tough ends snapped off and discarded, spears cut diagonally into 1-inch pieces

½ teaspoon grated lemon zest (from about ½ lemon)

1. Heat the oven to 425°. In a large roasting pan, toss the potatoes and garlic with 1½ tablespoons of the oil and ½ teaspoon salt. Put the pan in the upper third of the oven and cook, stirring once, for 15 minutes.

2. Meanwhile, coat the chicken with 1 tablespoon of the oil; arrange the pieces, skin-side up, in a smaller roasting pan. Sprinkle the chicken with the lemon juice, ¼ teaspoon salt, and ¼ teaspoon pepper. Top each piece of chicken with a piece of the butter.

3. Stir the potatoes. Put the chicken in the oven with the potatoes and cook for 10 minutes. Add the asparagus, the remaining 1 tablespoon oil, and ⅛ teaspoon each salt and pepper to the potatoes. Stir and continue cooking until the chicken, potatoes, and asparagus are done, 10 to 15 minutes longer. Remove both pans from the oven. Toss the potatoes and asparagus with the lemon zest. Serve with the chicken breasts.

PORK CHOPS WITH MUSHROOM BREAD PUDDING

Juices from the browned pork chops seep into the bread pudding, flavoring it as it bakes. We used one-inch-thick chops here. If yours are thicker, put them in the oven sooner rather than cooking the bread pudding longer, so the eggs don't curdle.

WINE RECOMMENDATION
Pork and mushrooms each have an incredible affinity for pinot noir, so this combination of the two makes for an easy choice. Favor a slightly earthy French Burgundy over its fruitier brethren from other countries. A premier cru wine offers complexity and concentrated fruit flavor; a village-level wine will be lighter and simpler.

SERVES 4

2 tablespoons butter

1 onion, chopped

1 rib celery, chopped

¾ pound mushrooms, cut into thin slices

1 teaspoon dried thyme

½ pound baguette (or other crusty bread), cut into ½-inch cubes (about 1 quart)

1 teaspoon salt

½ teaspoon fresh-ground black pepper

1⅓ cups canned low-sodium chicken broth or homemade stock

3 eggs, beaten to mix

⅔ cup half-and-half

1 tablespoon cooking oil

4 center-cut pork chops, about 1-inch thick (about 2 pounds in all)

1. Heat the oven to 325°. Butter a 9-by-13-inch baking dish or a gratin dish of similar size. In a large nonstick frying pan, melt the butter over moderately low heat. Add the onion and celery; cook, stirring occasionally, until starting to soften, about 3 minutes. Increase the heat to moderately high. Add the mushrooms and thyme and cook until the mushrooms start to brown, about 5 minutes. Remove the pan from the heat. Stir in the bread cubes, ¾ teaspoon of the salt, and ¼ teaspoon of the pepper. Transfer the mixture to the prepared baking dish.

2. Stir together the broth, eggs, and half-and-half. Pour the mixture evenly over the mushrooms and bread. Put the dish in the lower third of the oven and bake for 25 minutes.

3. Meanwhile, heat the oil in the frying pan over moderate heat. Sprinkle the remaining ¼ teaspoon each salt and pepper over the pork chops. Add the chops to the pan and brown, about 3 minutes per side. Remove the chops from the pan. Remove the bread pudding from the oven after it bakes for 25 minutes and set the pork chops directly on top. Return to the oven and cook until the meat is done and the pudding is just set, 10 to 15 minutes longer.

CANADIAN BACON, POTATO, AND SWISS-CHARD GRATIN

Grated Gruyère cheese melts among ribbons of leafy Swiss chard and slices of Canadian bacon and potato. The dish bakes until the cheese on top is a crusty golden brown.

WINE RECOMMENDATION
Merlot would be a marvelous choice to accompany this hearty dish. The wine has a fair amount of tannin, but that's easily handled by the bacon and cheese, which will accentuate the merlot's plummy flavor, too.

SERVES 4

2   tablespoons butter

½   pound Swiss chard, large stems removed, leaves cut crosswise into approximately 1-inch ribbons

1   clove garlic, minced

½   teaspoon salt

½   teaspoon fresh-ground black pepper

1½   pounds baking potatoes (about 2), peeled and cut into approximately ⅛-inch slices

¼   pound Gruyère, grated (about 1½ cups)

½   pound sliced Canadian bacon

⅔   cup canned low-sodium chicken broth or homemade stock

1. Heat the oven to 425°. In a medium frying pan, melt 1 tablespoon of the butter over moderately low heat. Add the Swiss chard and cook until starting to wilt, about 1 minute. Stir in the garlic and ⅛ teaspoon each salt and pepper.

Cook until no liquid remains in the pan, about 2 minutes.

2. Butter an 8-by-8-inch baking pan or similarly sized gratin dish. Layer one third of the potatoes in the dish and top with ⅛ teaspoon each salt and pepper, a third of the cheese, and half the Canadian bacon. Spread the Swiss chard in a single layer. Top with half the remaining potatoes and sprinkle with ⅛ teaspoon each salt and pepper. Spread half the remaining cheese and the remaining Canadian bacon over the potatoes. Add the remaining potatoes to the dish, sprinkle with the remaining ⅛ teaspoon each of salt and pepper, and top with the remaining cheese and 1 tablespoon butter. Pour the chicken broth over all.

3. Cover the gratin with aluminum foil and bake for 15 minutes. Remove the foil and continue baking until the potatoes are tender and the top is golden brown, about 30 minutes longer. Let stand 2 to 3 minutes before cutting.

MOUSSAKA

Our moussaka features two shortcuts, neither of which sacrifices flavor: The eggplant is broiled rather than fried, and the topping is a mixture of cheese and milk instead of the usual béchamel sauce. Watch the eggplant carefully while it cooks; if it burns it will taste bitter. Let the moussaka sit briefly before cutting it, so the squares will hold together.

WINE RECOMMENDATION
A lush California cabernet, with its black-currant and herb notes, will be a splendid match for this rich, spicy moussaka.

SERVES 4

6 tablespoons cooking oil

1 onion, chopped

2 cloves garlic, minced

1 pound ground lamb

$\frac{1}{2}$ cup red wine

1 tablespoon tomato paste

$1\frac{1}{2}$ cups canned crushed tomatoes in thick puree (one 15-ounce can)

1 bay leaf

1 cinnamon stick

$\frac{1}{8}$ teaspoon ground allspice

1 teaspoon salt

   Fresh-ground black pepper

1 eggplant (about 1 pound), peeled and cut into $\frac{1}{4}$-inch slices

4 ounces cream cheese

$\frac{1}{4}$ cup milk

$\frac{1}{4}$ cup grated Parmesan

1. Heat the broiler. In a large stainless-steel frying pan, heat 1 tablespoon of the oil over moderate heat. Add the onion and garlic; cook until starting to soften, about 3 minutes. Add the lamb and cook until the meat loses its pink color, about 2 minutes. Stir in the wine, tomato paste, tomatoes, bay leaf, cinnamon, allspice, $\frac{3}{4}$ teaspoon salt, and $\frac{1}{4}$ teaspoon pepper. Bring to a boil. Reduce the heat. Simmer, covered, for 10 minutes.

2. Brush both sides of the eggplant slices with the remaining 5 tablespoons oil and season with $\frac{1}{8}$ teaspoon each salt and pepper. Put the eggplant slices on a large baking sheet and broil, 6 inches from the heat, until browned, about 5 minutes. Turn and broil until browned on the other side, about 5 minutes longer.

3. In a small saucepan, combine the cream cheese, milk, $\frac{1}{8}$ teaspoon salt, and a pinch of pepper. Warm over low heat until just melted.

4. Oil an 8-by-8-inch baking dish. Layer half the eggplant in the dish, then half the meat sauce. Sprinkle with half the Parmesan. Repeat with the remaining eggplant, meat sauce, and Parmesan. Spoon the cream-cheese sauce on top; broil until just starting to brown, 1 to 2 minutes.

LAMB CHOPS WITH TOMATO-AND-POTATO GRATIN

Tomatoes, rather than cream or stock, provide the moisture in this gratin. Dried rosemary and thyme not only perfume the potatoes, but taste delicious with the lamb. If you like, use rib instead of loin chops.

WINE RECOMMENDATION
Bordeaux is the classic choice with lamb chops. Though our perceptions of Bordeaux are often distorted by the wildly expensive cru classé wines, many wines from the region are both affordable and delicious. Look for the appellations Bordeaux Supérieur, Bourg, Blaye, and Fronsac.

SERVES 4

3 tablespoons olive oil

2 onions, cut into thin slices

1 cup drained diced canned tomatoes

¾ teaspoon salt

¼ teaspoon dried rosemary, crumbled

¼ teaspoon dried thyme

¼ teaspoon fresh-ground black pepper

¼ cup grated Parmesan

1½ pounds baking potatoes (about 2), peeled and cut into approximately ⅛-inch slices

4 lamb loin chops, 1½ inches thick (about 1½ pounds in all), fat trimmed

1. Heat the oven to 450°. Oil an 8-by-11½-inch baking pan or similarly sized gratin dish. In a large nonstick frying pan, heat 2 tablespoons of the oil over moderately low heat. Add the onions and cook, stirring occasionally, until translucent, about 5 minutes. Remove the pan from the heat and stir in the tomatoes and ¼ teaspoon of the salt.

2. In a small bowl, combine the rosemary, thyme, ¼ teaspoon of the salt, ⅛ teaspoon of the pepper, and the Parmesan. Spread half the tomato-and-onion mixture in the bottom of the baking dish; layer half the potatoes on top. Sprinkle half the Parmesan mixture over the potatoes. Repeat with the remaining tomatoes and onions, potatoes, and Parmesan. Cover the dish with aluminum foil and bake for 30 minutes.

3. Meanwhile, wipe out the frying pan and then heat the remaining 1 tablespoon oil in it over moderate heat. Sprinkle the remaining ¼ teaspoon salt and ⅛ teaspoon pepper over the lamb chops. Cook until browned, about 3 minutes per side. Remove the chops from the pan.

4. Remove the baking dish from the oven and remove the aluminum foil. Put the lamb chops on top of the potatoes and return the dish to the oven. Cook until the meat and potatoes are just done, 10 to 12 minutes longer.

GRILLED SHRIMP AND PITAS WITH CHICKPEA PUREE

Canned chickpeas are delicious when mashed with garlic, lemon, olive oil, and parsley. Serve them with grilled shrimp and pitas for a quick Greek-inspired warm-weather dish.

WINE RECOMMENDATION
The ingredients here practically demand the citrus and herb flavors of a sauvignon blanc. A version from California will be a bit softer than the classic French Sancerre or Pouilly-Fumé, but in this case avoid wines labeled Fumé Blanc. Though also made from sauvignon blanc, they tend to be more oaky.

SERVES 4

1½   pounds large shrimp, shelled

9   tablespoons olive oil

½   teaspoon dried oregano

1   teaspoon salt

¼   teaspoon fresh-ground black pepper

2   cloves garlic, minced

4   cups drained and rinsed canned chickpeas (two 19-ounce cans)

¼   cup water

3   tablespoons lemon juice

3   tablespoons chopped flat-leaf parsley

4   pitas

4   tablespoons butter, at room temperature

1. Light the grill or heat the broiler. Thread the shrimp onto four skewers. Brush the shrimp with 2 tablespoons of the oil; sprinkle with the oregano, ¼ teaspoon of the salt, and the pepper.

2. In a medium saucepan, heat 5 tablespoons of the oil over moderately low heat. Add the garlic and cook, stirring, for 30 seconds. Add the chickpeas, water, and the remaining ¾ teaspoon of salt and heat until warmed through. With a potato masher, mash the chickpeas. Stir in 1 tablespoon of the lemon juice and the parsley. Cover to keep warm.

3. Grill or broil the shrimp, turning once, until just done, about 4 minutes in all. Meanwhile, spread both sides of each pita with the butter and grill or broil, turning once, until golden, about 4 minutes in all. Cut into quarters.

4. In a small glass or stainless-steel bowl, whisk together the remaining 2 tablespoons each of oil and lemon juice. Mound the chickpeas on plates. Top with the shrimp skewers and surround with the pita quarters. Pour the lemon oil over the shrimp and chickpeas.

105

GRILLED CORNISH HENS WITH WARM POTATO AND PORTOBELLO SALAD

The salad, tossed with just olive oil, garlic, and parsley, is simple as can be and really lets the flavor of Yukon Gold potatoes shine through. If you can't get these yellow potatoes, though, regular ones will do nicely.

WINE RECOMMENDATION
The clean, minerally taste of a chardonnay-based Mâcon-Villages or St-Véran from Burgundy will highlight the hens and potatoes.

SERVES 4

1¾ pounds boiling potatoes (about 5), preferably Yukon Gold

1½ pounds portobello mushrooms (about 4), stems removed

4 tablespoons cooking oil

1¼ teaspoons salt

¾ teaspoon fresh-ground black pepper

2 Cornish hens (about 1¼ pounds each), halved

⅓ cup olive oil

1 clove garlic, minced

½ cup chopped flat-leaf parsley

1. Put the potatoes in a medium saucepan of salted water. Bring to a boil, reduce the heat, and cook at a gentle boil until tender, about 30 minutes. Drain.

2. Meanwhile, light the grill. Coat the portobello caps with 2 tablespoons of the cooking oil and sprinkle with ¼ teaspoon of the salt and ¼ teaspoon of the pepper. Grill the portobellos, turning, until browned and just done, about 15 minutes. Remove.

3. Coat the hens with the remaining 2 tablespoons cooking oil. Sprinkle with ½ teaspoon of the salt and ¼ teaspoon of the pepper. Grill over moderate heat for 12 minutes. Turn and cook until just done, about 12 minutes longer.

4. When the potatoes and portobellos are cool enough to handle, peel the potatoes and cut them and the portobellos into ¼-inch slices. Put them in a large bowl and add the olive oil, garlic, parsley, and the remaining ½ teaspoon salt and ¼ teaspoon pepper. Mound on plates and top with the hens.

TEST-KITCHEN TIP

We like extra-virgin olive oil in this potato salad, but sometimes it's so powerful that it overwhelms the potatoes. If yours is strong, mix it half and half with a less exalted oil.

GRILLED SPICE-RUBBED PORK TENDERLOIN WITH SWEET POTATOES AND SCALLIONS

Cook a whole meal—meat, potatoes, and a vegetable—on the grill. The pork tenderloin is coated in a sweet-and-spicy paste that's similar to Jamaican jerk marinade. Scallions, not often served as a cooked vegetable, deserve to be used as more than a raw garnish.

WINE RECOMMENDATION
Australian Shiraz's lush, jammy fruit flavor makes it a great partner for grilled meats. Try one here for an inexpensive but tasty treat.

SERVES 4

5	tablespoons cooking oil
1/4	teaspoon cayenne
1	teaspoon dried thyme
1/8	teaspoon nutmeg
1	tablespoon brown sugar
1/2	teaspoon wine vinegar
1	teaspoon salt
	Fresh-ground black pepper
1 1/2	pounds pork tenderloin
1 1/2	pounds sweet potatoes, peeled and cut diagonally into 1/4-inch slices
12	scallions including 2 inches of green top, root end trimmed

1. Light the grill. In a small bowl, combine 3 tablespoons of the oil with the cayenne, thyme, nutmeg, brown sugar, vinegar, 3/4 teaspoon of the salt, and 1/4 teaspoon black pepper. Rub the mixture over the pork.

2. Bring a medium pot of water to a boil. Add the sweet potatoes and cook until almost tender, about 5 minutes. Drain. Brush the sweet potatoes and the scallions with the remaining 2 tablespoons oil and sprinkle with the remaining 1/4 teaspoon salt and 1/8 teaspoon pepper.

3. Grill the pork over moderate heat, turning once, until done to medium, 12 to 15 minutes in all. Transfer the pork to a carving board and leave to rest in a warm spot.

4. Grill the sweet potatoes and scallions, turning, until tender, about 5 minutes. Cut the pork into 1/2-inch diagonal slices. Serve with the vegetables.

VARIATION

Substitute 1 pound of **asparagus spears** for the scallions. Snap off the tough ends and use an additional tablespoon of oil for brushing the spears. Grill for about 10 minutes.

GRILLED STEAK OVER BLACK BEANS WITH CHIMICHURRI SAUCE

In South America, piquant *chimichurri* sauce is a favorite accompaniment to grilled meats. Serve bread alongside to soak up the sauce; you won't want to miss a drop.

WINE RECOMMENDATION
This robust dish needs a rollicking red. Go for an all-American Napa, Sonoma, or Amador zinfandel for spiciness and big fruit flavor.

SERVES 4

2 tablespoons cooking oil

1 onion, chopped

3 cloves garlic, minced

3 cups drained and rinsed canned black beans (from two 15-ounce cans)

1 cup canned low-sodium chicken broth or homemade stock

⅔ cup canned crushed tomatoes in thick puree

1 7-ounce jar sliced pimentos, drained (⅔ cup)

1 bay leaf

1 teaspoon salt

1½ pounds sirloin steak, about 1 inch thick

¼ teaspoon fresh-ground black pepper

   Chimichurri Sauce, right

1. In a medium saucepan, heat 1 tablespoon of the oil over moderately low heat. Add the onion and garlic and cook, stirring occasionally, until translucent, about 5 minutes. Add the beans, broth, tomatoes, pimentos, bay leaf, and ½ teaspoon of the salt. Simmer until thickened, about 20 minutes. Remove the bay leaf.

2. Light the grill or heat the broiler. Rub the steak with the remaining oil; sprinkle with the remaining salt and the pepper. Grill or broil for 4 minutes. Turn; cook to your taste, about 4 minutes longer for medium-rare. Cut into thin diagonal slices. Top the beans with the steak and sauce.

CHIMICHURRI SAUCE

MAKES ABOUT 1 CUP

1 cup lightly packed fresh parsley leaves

2 large cloves garlic, smashed

1 teaspoon dried thyme

¼ teaspoon dried red-pepper flakes

½ cup water

¼ cup red-wine vinegar

¼ cup olive oil

½ teaspoon salt

⅛ teaspoon fresh-ground black pepper

Put all the ingredients in the blender. Puree until almost smooth.

Stovetop Cooking

SZECHUAN SHRIMP

Traditional Szechuan dishes are often quite spicy, but we've given this recipe only a slight dose of heat. If your taste runs to the incendiary, make yours hotter by adding more red-pepper flakes.

WINE RECOMMENDATION
A German riesling will be a knockout here. If you're keeping the heat subdued, a Pfalz kabinett will work fine. If you increase the pepper, go to a sweeter spätlese or even an auslese.

SERVES 4

½ cup canned low-sodium chicken broth or homemade stock

3 tablespoons ketchup

1½ tablespoons soy sauce

1 tablespoon oyster sauce

¼ teaspoon salt

3 tablespoons sherry

2 red bell peppers, cut into ¾-inch pieces

1¼ cups long-grain rice

1½ pounds medium shrimp, shelled

½ teaspoon cornstarch

3 tablespoons cooking oil

3 cloves garlic, minced

1 tablespoon minced fresh ginger

2 scallions, white part chopped, green tops sliced

½ teaspoon dried red-pepper flakes

½ teaspoon Asian sesame oil

1. In a small bowl, combine the chicken broth, ketchup, soy sauce, oyster sauce, salt, and 1 tablespoon of the sherry. Heat a wok or large frying pan over moderately high heat until very hot. Add the bell peppers and stir-fry until starting to blacken, about 5 minutes. Remove.

2. Bring a medium pot of salted water to a boil. Stir in the rice and boil until just done, about 10 minutes. Drain.

3. Meanwhile, toss the shrimp with the remaining 2 tablespoons sherry and the cornstarch. Heat 1½ tablespoons of the oil in the wok or frying pan over moderately high heat. Add the shrimp and stir-fry until just done, 3 to 4 minutes. Remove the shrimp and add the remaining 1½ tablespoons oil. Reduce the heat to moderate and add the charred bell peppers, the garlic, ginger, the chopped scallions, and the red-pepper flakes. Cook, stirring, until soft, about 3 minutes.

4. Increase the heat to high. Add the broth mixture and boil until thickened, about 2 minutes. Add the shrimp and sliced scallions and just heat through. Drizzle the sesame oil over the top. Serve the shrimp with the rice.

SCALLOP-TOPPED POTATO AND CELERY-ROOT PUREE WITH LEMON BROWN-BUTTER SAUCE

The addition of celery root gives mashed potatoes an extra, surprisingly herbal dimension. The puree provides a perfect nest for seared scallops, and a drizzle of simple but intensely flavored sauce completes this delectable dish. It will make you feel you're dining in a multi-starred restaurant.

WINE RECOMMENDATION
A white wine with full flavor makes a fine partner for scallops; on the other hand, a wine with some acidity is good, too. Try a crisp and minerally Chablis, made entirely from chardonnay, for the best of both.

SERVES 4

1½ pounds baking potatoes (about 3), peeled and cut into 2-inch chunks

1 pound celery root, peeled and cut into 2-inch chunks

Salt

Fresh-ground black pepper

8 tablespoons butter, at room temperature

1 tablespoon cooking oil

2 pounds sea scallops

3 tablespoons chopped flat-leaf parsley

1 tablespoon drained capers

1 teaspoon lemon juice

1. Put the potatoes and celery root in a medium saucepan of salted water. Bring to a boil, reduce the heat, and cook at a low boil until tender, about 20 minutes.

2. Reserve ½ cup of the cooking water, and then drain the potatoes and celery root. Put them back into the saucepan along with ¼ teaspoon salt and a pinch of pepper. Mash over very low heat, incorporating the reserved cooking water and 5 tablespoons of the butter.

3. In a large nonstick frying pan, heat ½ tablespoon of the oil over moderately high heat. Season the scallops with ¼ teaspoon salt and ¼ teaspoon pepper. Add half the scallops to the pan. Cook until browned, about 2 minutes. Turn and cook until browned on the second side and just done, about 1 minute. Remove. Heat the remaining ½ tablespoon oil in the pan and cook the remaining scallops. Remove.

4. Reduce the heat to moderate. Add the remaining 3 tablespoons butter to the pan and cook until golden, about 2 minutes. Add the scallops and any accumulated juices, the parsley, capers, lemon juice, and ⅛ teaspoon salt. Mound the puree on plates and top with the scallops and sauce.

RED SNAPPER ON RICE WITH RED-CURRY CARROT SAUCE

Red Thai curry paste gives this pureed carrot sauce spiciness and depth of flavor. The sweetness of the carrots along with a touch of brown sugar balances the heat but in no way erases it. Use less curry paste if you prefer.

WINE RECOMMENDATION
Very few wines mesh as well with Asian spiciness as riesling; it's the clear choice here. Go for an off-dry one from Washington State.

SERVES 4

1   cup jasmine or other long-grain rice

1½   cups water

¾   pound carrots (about 4), cut into ¼-inch pieces

1   clove garlic, smashed

2½   cups canned low-sodium chicken broth or homemade stock

1¼   cups whole milk

1½   tablespoons Asian fish sauce (nam pla or nuoc mam)*

1½   teaspoons red Thai curry paste*

1¾   teaspoons brown sugar

¾   teaspoon salt

1   tablespoon cooking oil

2   pounds red snapper fillets

⅓   cup cilantro leaves (optional)

     Lime wedges, for serving

     *Available at Asian markets and many supermarkets

1. Rinse the rice until the water runs clear. Put the rice in a small saucepan with the water. Bring to a boil, reduce the heat to low, and cook, covered, for 15 minutes. Remove the pan from the heat and let sit, without removing the lid, for 10 minutes.

2. Meanwhile, in a medium saucepan, bring the carrots, garlic, and broth to a boil. Cook, covered, over moderately low heat until the carrots are tender, about 15 minutes. Puree the carrots, garlic, and broth in a blender and pour back into the pan. Add the milk, fish sauce, curry paste, brown sugar, and ½ teaspoon of the salt and bring to a simmer, stirring occasionally.

3. In a large nonstick frying pan, heat the oil over moderately high heat. Season the fish with the remaining ¼ teaspoon salt. Cook the fish, skin-side down, until golden, about 4 minutes. Turn, reduce the heat to moderate, and continue cooking until just done, about 4 minutes longer for 1-inch-thick fillets. Mound the rice on plates and top with the fish and the sauce. Sprinkle with the cilantro, if using, and serve with the lime wedges.

PASTA SALAD WITH SEARED TUNA AND CITRUS DRESSING

Here's an ideal warm-weather meal with the refreshing flavors of mint, orange, lemon, and cucumber. Tuna, hot from the pan, is cut into chunks and tossed with the room-temperature pasta salad. You could also cook the tuna outside on the grill.

WINE RECOMMENDATION
Whether you make this salad with tuna or one of the alternatives listed in the box below, a dry riesling from Alsace will be splendid. Its lime, mineral, and herbal notes will brilliantly echo the salad and set off the fish.

SERVES 4

½ pound spaghettini

2 tablespoons red-wine vinegar

½ teaspoon grated orange zest (from about ¼ orange)

1 tablespoon fresh orange juice

1 tablespoon lemon juice

1 teaspoon Dijon mustard

Salt

Fresh-ground black pepper

6½ tablespoons olive oil

2 cucumbers, peeled, halved lengthwise, seeded, and cut crosswise into thin slices

6 tablespoons chopped fresh mint

1 pound tuna steak, about 1 inch thick

1. In a large pot of boiling, salted water, cook the spaghettini until just done, about 9 minutes. Drain. Rinse with cold water; drain thoroughly.

2. In a large glass or stainless-steel bowl, whisk together the vinegar, orange zest, orange juice, lemon juice, mustard, ¾ teaspoon salt, and ¼ teaspoon pepper. Add 6 tablespoons of the oil slowly, whisking. Add the spaghettini, cucumbers, and mint and toss.

3. Heat a grill pan or heavy frying pan over moderately high heat. Coat the tuna with the remaining ½ tablespoon oil and sprinkle with ⅛ teaspoon salt and a pinch of pepper. Cook, turning once, until done to your taste, about 2 minutes per side for medium rare. Remove. Cut the tuna into 1-inch chunks and toss with the spaghettini.

FISH ALTERNATIVES

You could use salmon fillets or swordfish steaks in place of the tuna. For either, add a few minutes to the cooking time.

CHICKEN CHILAQUILES

Tortilla chips heated in a quick-cooking chile sauce and topped with feta, onion, sour cream, cilantro, and chicken make a particularly tasty version of this popular Mexican dish. Don't let the idea of softened chips put you off. This recipe is a winner.

WINE RECOMMENDATION
These forceful, varied flavors need a gutsy wine, and zinfandel will more than hold its own. Look for old-vine cuvées from Sonoma's Dry Creek or Russian River valleys.

SERVES 4

3½ tablespoons paprika

2½ tablespoons chili powder

½ teaspoon cayenne

¼ teaspoon ground cumin

1 teaspoon sugar

½ teaspoon salt

3 tablespoons cooking oil

3 tablespoons flour

2 cloves garlic, minced

3 cups canned low-sodium chicken broth or homemade stock

1⅓ pounds boneless, skinless chicken breasts (about 4 in all)

¼ teaspoon fresh-ground black pepper

½ pound tortilla chips

¼ pound feta, crumbled (about ¾ cup)

½ cup sour cream

1 red onion, sliced thin

½ cup cilantro leaves

1. In a small bowl, combine the paprika, chili powder, cayenne, cumin, sugar, and ¼ teaspoon of the salt.

2. In a large saucepan, heat 2 tablespoons of the oil over moderately low heat. Add the flour and cook, whisking, until golden, about 3 minutes. Add the garlic; cook for 30 seconds. Add the paprika and chili powder mixture and then add the broth slowly, whisking, until smooth. Bring to a simmer. Simmer, covered, until thick enough to coat a spoon, about 25 minutes.

3. Meanwhile, in a large frying pan, heat the remaining 1 tablespoon oil over moderate heat. Season the chicken with the remaining ¼ teaspoon salt and the pepper and cook until browned and just done, about 5 minutes per side. Remove the chicken from the pan and let it rest for 5 minutes. Cut crosswise into slices.

4. Add the tortilla chips to the chile sauce and cook, stirring, until the chips are soft but not falling apart, about 2 minutes. Put the sauce on plates and top with the feta, sour cream, onion, cilantro, and chicken.

CAPER-STUFFED VEAL WITH TOMATO SPINACH SAUCE

Veal rolls are filled with a mixture of capers, bread crumbs, and parsley for an easy and elegant entrée. Wilted spinach leaves add interest to the winey tomato sauce.

WINE RECOMMENDATION
Dolcetto d'Alba may taste too tart when drunk on its own, but it will shine when balanced by a tomato sauce such as the one here.

SERVES 4

¼ cup drained capers

2 tablespoons chopped fresh parsley

⅓ cup dry bread crumbs

½ teaspoon anchovy paste

4 tablespoons olive oil

8 veal scaloppine (about 1½ pounds in all)
  Salt
  Fresh-ground black pepper

1 tablespoon butter

½ cup red wine

1½ cups canned crushed tomatoes in thick puree (one 15-ounce can)

10 ounces spinach, large stems removed, leaves washed

1. In a small bowl, combine the capers, parsley, bread crumbs, anchovy paste, and 2 tablespoons of the olive oil.

2. Put the veal on a work surface and sprinkle ⅛ teaspoon salt and ⅛ teaspoon pepper over the meat. Put some of the stuffing near the bottom of each piece of veal. Roll the veal up loosely, enclosing the stuffing, and secure each piece with a toothpick.

3. In a large deep frying pan, heat the remaining 2 tablespoons oil and the butter over moderate heat. Add the veal rolls to the pan and brown, in batches if necessary, for about 3 minutes. Remove.

4. Reduce the heat to moderately low. Add the wine to the pan and cook, stirring to dislodge any brown bits that cling to the bottom of the pan. Stir in the tomatoes, ½ teaspoon salt, and ¼ teaspoon pepper. Bring to a simmer. Return the veal to the pan. Cover and continue to simmer, turning the rolls once, until tender, about 25 minutes.

5. Remove the veal from the pan. Add the spinach to the sauce and simmer until the spinach wilts and the sauce thickens, about 3 minutes. Remove the toothpicks from the veal rolls and serve the rolls with the sauce.

POTATO, SALAMI, AND CHEESE FRITTATA

Fortified with sautéed potatoes, strips of salami, and bits of goat cheese, this robust egg dish makes a fine dinner. Add a salad and you're all set. Though we like them warm, frittatas are traditionally served at room temperature.

WINE RECOMMENDATION
Accompany the rich frittata with a chardonnay from South Africa. Their wines tend to be French in style, with more acidity and less fruitness than those from the United States.

SERVES 4

2	tablespoons cooking oil
1	½-pound baking potato, peeled and cut into ½-inch cubes
¼	teaspoon salt
8	large eggs
⅛	teaspoon fresh-ground black pepper
¼	cup grated Parmesan
3	ounces sliced hard salami, slices halved and then cut crosswise into thin strips
1	tablespoon butter
¼	pound mild goat cheese such as Montrachet, crumbled

1. In a 12-inch nonstick ovenproof frying pan or cast-iron pan, heat 1 tablespoon of the oil over moderate heat. Add the potato and salt and sauté until the potato cubes are brown and just done, about 5 minutes. Remove from the pan and let cool.

2. In a large bowl, beat the eggs with the pepper and Parmesan. Stir in the salami and the potato.

3. Add the butter and the remaining 1 tablespoon oil to the pan. Melt the butter over moderate heat. Pour the egg mixture in the pan and reduce the heat to low. Sprinkle the goat cheese over the top. Cook until the eggs are nearly set, 6 to 7 minutes.

4. Heat the broiler. Broil the frittata 6 inches from the heat, if possible, until the eggs are set, about 2 minutes. Loosen the frittata with a spatula and slide the frittata onto a plate. Cut into wedges and serve.

TEST-KITCHEN TIP

If the handle of your frying pan isn't oven-proof, protect it from the heat of the broiler with about four layers of aluminum foil.

LENTILS WITH SMOKED SAUSAGE AND CARROTS

A good-quality, at least slightly hot mustard from France, Germany, or England is the perfect accompaniment for this. Put a dollop on your plate and dip each forkful into it.

WINE RECOMMENDATION

Tokay Pinot Gris is one of the few white wines big enough to partner dishes that might ordinarily call for a red. Here its full body is more than a match for the sausage, while its nutty notes intriguingly echo the lentils.

SERVES 4

- 2 tablespoons cooking oil
- 1 onion, chopped
- 3 cloves garlic, minced
- 3 carrots, halved lengthwise and cut crosswise into ¾-inch pieces
- 1 pound lentils (about 2⅓ cups)
- 1 quart water
- 1¼ teaspoons salt
- 1 bay leaf
- 1 teaspoon dried thyme
- 1 pound smoked sausage, cut diagonally into ¾-inch slices
- 3 tablespoons chopped fresh parsley

1. In a large saucepan, heat the oil over moderately low heat. Add the onion, garlic, and carrots. Cook, stirring occasionally, until the onion is translucent, about 5 minutes.

2. Add the lentils, water, salt, bay leaf, and thyme. Bring to a boil, reduce the heat, and simmer, partially covered, until the lentils are almost tender, about 20 minutes. Discard the bay leaf.

3. Stir in the smoked sausage and parsley. Cook until the lentils are just tender but not falling apart and the sausage is warm, about 10 minutes longer.

COOKING LENTILS

Because salt retards the cooking of legumes, the general wisdom is not to add it until they're almost done. Lentils, however, tend to overcook and fall apart all too quickly, so we put the salt in at the outset.

PICADILLO

Our version of this Cuban classic mixes ground beef with a highly seasoned tomato sauce, fried potatoes, raisins, and green olives. *Picadillo*, which should be only slightly saucy, often fills empanadas or soft tacos. We like it with corn bread or warm flour tortillas.

WINE RECOMMENDATION

Northern Rhône reds need robust culinary foils, and this sturdy *picadillo* is up to the task. Look for a St-Joseph or Crozes-Hermitage—or, if you want to splurge, a Hermitage or Côte Rôtie. If you don't, a beer will be just fine.

SERVES 4

1¼ pounds ground beef

1 large onion, chopped

1 green bell pepper, chopped

2 cloves garlic, minced

½ cup beer

1⅓ cups drained canned chopped tomatoes (one 15-ounce can)

2 tablespoons tomato paste

2 teaspoons ground cumin

1¼ teaspoons ground coriander

1½ teaspoons salt

¼ teaspoon fresh-ground black pepper

¼ teaspoon Tabasco sauce

2 tablespoons cooking oil

1 pound baking potatoes (about 2), peeled and cut into ½-inch pieces

½ cup raisins

½ cup quartered and pitted green olives

1. In a large stainless-steel frying pan, cook the ground beef until it is no longer pink. Add the onion, bell pepper, and garlic and cook, stirring occasionally, until starting to soften, about 3 minutes.

2. Stir in the beer, tomatoes, tomato paste, cumin, coriander, salt, black pepper, and Tabasco sauce and bring to a boil. Reduce the heat and simmer, covered, for 15 minutes.

3. Meanwhile, in a large nonstick frying pan, heat the oil over moderately high heat. Add the potatoes and cook, stirring occasionally, until golden brown, 8 to 10 minutes.

4. Add the potatoes, raisins, and olives to the meat mixture. Cook, covered, until the potatoes are just done, about 10 minutes longer.

SUKIYAKI

A delicious mixture of beef, noodles, Chinese cabbage, spinach, and tofu, sukiyaki is easy to make. Japan has excellent well-marbled beef that's used for this specialty, so you'll need a good cut to get a similar flavor. We find that club steak works well. Have your butcher cut it as thin as possible. We use angel hair in place of traditional Asian transparent noodles, but you could certainly include them if they're available to you.

WINE RECOMMENDATION
A good lager will probably be the best choice, but if you want to be adventurous, try a pinot noir from California. More overtly fruity than its Burgundian counterparts, it will marry effectively with the soup.

SERVES 4

½ pound angel hair

3 tablespoons cooking oil

¼ cup sugar

1½ pounds club steak, trimmed of fat, sliced very thin

10 scallions including green tops, cut diagonally into 1-inch lengths

¾ cup canned low-sodium chicken broth or homemade stock

⅔ cup soy sauce

⅓ cup sake or dry white wine

½ pound soft tofu, drained and cut into ¼-inch cubes

½ pound napa cabbage, cut into 1-inch pieces

¼ pound mushrooms, quartered

½ pound spinach, large stems removed and leaves washed

1. In a large pot of boiling, salted water, cook the pasta until just done, about 3 minutes. Drain. Rinse with cold water and drain thoroughly.

2. Heat a large nonstick frying pan over moderately high heat. Add the oil and sprinkle the sugar into the pan. Let sit until the sugar begins to turn golden brown, about 1 minute. Stir until the sugar turns a medium brown. Add the steak, in about five batches, turning quickly with tongs, until browned and just done, 1 or 2 minutes in all. Remove. The sugar should glaze the beef with brown caramel. If the pan gets too hot, reduce the heat to moderate so the sugar won't burn. Add the scallions; cook, stirring, until browned, about 2 minutes.

3. In the pasta-cooking pot, combine the pasta, the beef and any accumulated juices, the scallions, broth, soy sauce, sake, tofu, cabbage, and mushrooms and bring to a simmer. Simmer, stirring, until the vegetables are almost tender, about 2 minutes. Add the spinach and continue cooking until wilted, about 30 seconds longer.

CALF'S LIVER WITH SPINACH SALAD, CROUTONS, AND PINE NUTS

The secret to great calf's liver is simple: don't overcook it. If you do, it will most assuredly be dry, tough, and generally worthy of the cold shoulder it too often gets. Here sautéed calf's liver sits on a bed of spinach salad tossed with grainy-mustard dressing.

WINE RECOMMENDATION
Though the cabernet-franc-based reds of the Loire Valley are virtually ignored in the United States, their berry-like flavor, medium body, and crisp texture are often more versatile with food than their heavier Bordeaux brethren. A Saumur-Champigny will be lovely here.

SERVES 4

- 3 tablespoons pine nuts
- 1 ¾-pound loaf country bread, cut into ¾-inch cubes
- 2 tablespoons wine vinegar
- 1 tablespoon grainy mustard
- 1 teaspoon salt
- ½ teaspoon fresh-ground black pepper
- 6 tablespoons olive oil
- ¼ cup flour
- 1 tablespoon butter
- 4 slices calf's liver (about 1½ pounds in all)
- 1 pound spinach, large stems removed and leaves washed (about 9 cups)

1. Heat the oven to 350°. Toast the pine nuts in the oven until golden brown, about 5 minutes. Toast the bread cubes in the oven until golden but still slightly soft in the center, about 15 minutes.

2. In a small glass or stainless-steel bowl, whisk together the vinegar, mustard, ½ teaspoon of the salt, and ¼ teaspoon of the pepper. Add 5 tablespoons of the oil slowly, whisking.

3. Combine the flour with the remaining ½ teaspoon salt and ¼ teaspoon pepper. In a large frying pan, heat the remaining 1 tablespoon oil and the butter over moderate heat. Dust the liver slices with the flour mixture and shake off the excess. Put the liver in the pan and cook until browned, about 3 minutes. Turn and cook until browned on the other side, 3 to 4 minutes longer. It should still be pink in the center. Remove.

4. In a large bowl, toss the spinach with all but 2 tablespoons of the dressing. Add the croutons and pine nuts and toss. Mound the spinach on plates and top with the liver. Drizzle with the reserved dressing.

Pizzas, Sandwiches, Etc.

SUMMER PIZZA

Use the best tomatoes you can find for this seasonal pizza. To avoid a soggy crust, we recommend salting and draining the tomatoes to get rid of some of their juice.

Bardolino and Valpolicella are made for fresh tomatoey pizza and warm summer days. Among the world's most popular wines, these sprightly reds from Italy's Veneto are based on the corvina grape. Valpolicella is the richer of the two; Bardolino is almost rosé-like in its delicacy.

SERVES 4

- 4 tomatoes (about 2 pounds), seeded and chopped
- 1 teaspoon salt
- 1 small red onion, cut into thin slices
- 10 ounces fresh mozzarella, cut into small cubes (about 2 cups)
- 6 tablespoons chopped fresh basil
- ¼ teaspoon fresh-ground black pepper
- 2 12-inch store-bought pizza shells, such as Boboli
- ½ cup grated Parmesan
- 2 tablespoons olive oil

1. Heat the oven to 450°. Put the tomatoes in a strainer set over a medium bowl. Toss with the salt and let drain for 15 minutes.

2. In a medium bowl, combine the drained tomatoes with the onion, mozzarella, basil, and pepper. Top each pizza shell with half of the tomato mixture.

3. Sprinkle the pizzas with the Parmesan and drizzle with the oil. Bake directly on the oven rack until the cheese just melts, about 8 minutes.

GRILLED PIZZA

The summer ingredients on this pizza make it a perfect candidate for grilling. Brush a tablespoon of oil on the top of the pizza shells and set them, oiled-side down, on the grill. Cook until warm, about three minutes. Brush with another tablespoon of oil, flip the shells, and top with the remaining ingredients. Cook until the cheese just melts, about ten minutes.

Clam Pizza with Salad Topping

We've always secretly liked scooping up a bite of salad with a piece of pizza, and lately the idea of mounding dressed greens on top of pizza has caught on with hot chefs, too.

WINE RECOMMENDATION
Pinot grigio outsells other white wines in Italian restaurants by more than two to one, and this is the kind of dish that really shows why. Crisp, clean, and light, a good pinot grigio will nicely highlight the clams and tomatoes.

SERVES 4

20 ounces store-bought pizza dough

1 pound chopped clams, drained well (about 2 cups), or 4 dozen littlenecks, shucked and drained well

4 cloves garlic, minced

¼ teaspoon dried red-pepper flakes

½ teaspoon salt

4 tablespoons olive oil

2 quarts mixed salad greens (about 6 ounces)

¾ cup halved cherry tomatoes (about ¼ pound)

1½ teaspoons wine vinegar

¼ teaspoon fresh-ground black pepper

1. Heat the oven to 425°. Oil two 12-inch pizza pans or large baking sheets. Press the pizza dough into an approximately 12-inch round, or 9-by-13-inch rectangle, on each prepared pan. Bake until the dough begins to brown, about 10 minutes.

2. Meanwhile, line a strainer with several paper towels. Put the drained clams in the strainer and press gently to remove excess moisture.

3. Spread the clams on the partially baked pizza crusts, sprinkle with the garlic, red-pepper flakes, and ¼ teaspoon of the salt, and drizzle with 3 tablespoons of the oil. Bake the pizzas for 8 to 10 minutes. Do not overcook or the clams will toughen.

4. Meanwhile, in a large bowl, toss the greens with the cherry tomatoes, the remaining 1 tablespoon oil, the vinegar, the remaining ¼ teaspoon salt, and the black pepper. Remove the pizzas from the oven and top with the salad.

Plenty of Dough

If you're unable to find pizza dough in the refrigerator section of your supermarket, pizza places will often sell it to you by the pound. Just ask.

SUN-DRIED-TOMATO, SAUSAGE, AND FONTINA PIZZA

Topped with fennel-scented Italian sausage, sliced fontina, and strips of sun-dried tomatoes, a prepared pizza shell from the supermarket becomes an irresistible supper, needing nothing more than a simple green salad on the side.

WINE RECOMMENDATION
This pizza works well with either a white or red wine, but a pinot grigio is the best choice to echo the sausage's fennel and the fontina. Pinot grigios have slight apple and nut flavors and enough acidity to leave the palate refreshed.

SERVES 4

1 pound sweet Italian sausage, casings removed

²⁄₃ cup chopped drained oil-packed sun-dried tomatoes, plus ¼ cup of the oil

2 12-inch store-bought pizza shells, such as Boboli

½ pound fontina, cut into thin slices

¼ cup grated Parmesan

1. Heat the oven to 450°. In a large frying pan, cook the sausage over moderate heat, breaking it up with a fork or wooden spoon, until cooked through and just beginning to brown, about 10 minutes.

2. Brush the sun-dried-tomato oil over the pizza shells. Spread the sausage over the pizza shells. Scatter the sun-dried tomatoes over the sausage, put the fontina on top, and sprinkle the Parmesan over all.

3. Bake the pizzas, directly on the oven rack (for a crisper crust) or on two baking sheets, until the cheese is melted, about 10 minutes.

PIZZA CRUSTS

Prebaked pizza shells offer a fantastic way to make quick weeknight pizzas. You can even keep them in the freezer for last-minute meals. If the shell is still frozen, either add five minutes to the cooking time or pop the naked shell in the oven for five minutes before topping it. If you prefer to start with store-bought pizza dough or your own home-made pizza dough, simply follow the instructions in Step 1 of the recipe for Clam Pizza with Salad Topping, page 141, to prebake the crust before topping it.

SHRIMP PO' BOYS

Crisp fried shrimp are stuffed into a hollowed-out baguette that's been buttered, toasted, and spread with a zesty sauce. Use more Tabasco in the sauce to suit your taste, or pass the bottle at the table so fire lovers can sprinkle it directly on their sandwiches.

WINE RECOMMENDATION
Choose a cold beer rather than wine. It's the best choice for washing down these spicy sandwiches.

SERVES 4

4   6-inch lengths baguette, split

2   tablespoons butter, at room temperature

⅔   cup mayonnaise

2½ tablespoons Dijon mustard

¼   teaspoon Tabasco sauce, more to taste
    Cooking oil, for frying

½   cup whole milk

1   egg, beaten to mix

¾   cup dry bread crumbs

½   teaspoon salt

¼   teaspoon fresh-ground black pepper

¼   teaspoon cayenne

1¼ pounds large shrimp, shelled

⅓   cup flour

2   cups shredded romaine or iceberg lettuce

1   tomato, cut into thin slices

1. Heat the oven to 350°. Remove the soft centers of the baguette, leaving a ½-inch shell. Put the bread, cut-side up, on a baking sheet and brush with the butter. In a small bowl, combine the mayonnaise, mustard, and Tabasco sauce.

2. Heat about 3 inches of oil in a medium saucepan until it reaches approximately 360°. In a medium bowl, combine the milk and the egg. In another bowl, combine the bread crumbs with the salt, black pepper, and cayenne. Dip the shrimp into the flour, then into the egg mixture, and then into the bread crumbs.

3. Put about a third of the breaded shrimp into the oil and fry, turning, until golden on the outside and just done in the center, 2 to 3 minutes. Drain on paper towels. Repeat with the remaining two batches of shrimp.

4. Meanwhile, bake the pieces of baguette until crisp, about 5 minutes. Spread the sauce on both sides of the bread. Sandwich the lettuce, tomato, and fried shrimp between the bread.

CHICKEN PARMESAN HEROES

Hero sandwiches at the sub shop are usually served on untoasted rolls, but we prefer to brush the bread with olive oil and run it under the broiler for a minute or two. If you like, put a slice of mozzarella on the top half of each before broiling.

WINE RECOMMENDATION
A simple wine befits a simple dish. Select a fresh, grapey Chianti to drink with these homey Italian-American heroes.

SERVES 4

½ cup dry bread crumbs

½ cup grated Parmesan

1¼ teaspoons salt

½ teaspoon fresh-ground black pepper

3 tablespoons olive oil

1 onion, minced

2 cloves garlic, minced

2⅓ cups canned crushed tomatoes in thick puree (from a 28-ounce can)

Pinch dried red-pepper flakes (optional)

Cooking oil, for frying

4 boneless, skinless chicken breasts (about 1⅓ pounds in all)

2 eggs, beaten to mix

4 small (about 6 inches) hero or other sandwich rolls, split

1. In a shallow bowl, combine the bread crumbs, Parmesan, ½ teaspoon of the salt, and ¼ teaspoon of the black pepper.

2. In a large saucepan, heat 1 tablespoon of the olive oil over moderately low heat. Add the onion and cook, stirring occasionally, until translucent, about 5 minutes. Add the garlic and stir for 30 seconds. Stir in the tomatoes, red-pepper flakes, and the remaining ¾ teaspoon salt and ¼ teaspoon black pepper. Bring to a simmer, reduce the heat, and simmer, stirring occasionally, until thickened, about 20 minutes. Remove from the heat and cover to keep warm.

3. Meanwhile, in a large frying pan, heat ¼ to ½ inch of cooking oil over moderate heat until very hot. Dip each chicken breast into the eggs and then into the bread crumbs, coating well. Fry in the hot oil, turning once, until golden brown and just cooked through, about 15 minutes in all. Drain on paper towels.

4. While the chicken is cooking, heat the broiler. Brush the remaining 2 tablespoons olive oil over the cut-side of the rolls and toast under the broiler until golden, about 2 minutes. Spoon half the tomato sauce onto the bottom half of the rolls. Top with the chicken, the remaining sauce, and the other half of the rolls.

HOT MUFFULETTA

Before the hard salami, ham, and provolone are piled on, the bread for these New Orleans sandwiches is spread with a piquant olive salad flavored with garlic, oregano, and fresh parsley.

WINE RECOMMENDATION
Beaujolais has been called the perfect pic-nic wine. An exuberantly fruity bottle suits this jazzed-up ham-and-cheese sandwich perfectly.

SERVES 4

1	10-ounce jar green olives with pimientos, drained and chopped
1½	teaspoons dried oregano
1	clove garlic, minced
3	tablespoons olive oil
¼	cup chopped fresh parsley
4	large, crusty rolls, split
½	pound sliced hard salami
½	pound sliced ham
½	pound sliced provolone

1. Heat the oven to 350°. In a small bowl, combine the chopped olives with the oregano, garlic, oil, and parsley. Spread some of the olive mixture on the bottom half of each roll.

2. Top the olive salad with the salami, ham, and provolone. Cover with the tops of the rolls and then wrap each sandwich in aluminum foil. Bake until the cheese melts, about 15 minutes.

VARIATIONS

■ Instead of heating the sandwiches, serve them the more traditional way—at **room temperature**.

■ Use a combination of chopped, pitted **black olives**, such as Kalamata, and green olives with pimientos in the salad for both color and flavor.

BARBECUED-PORK BURRITOS WITH CHOPPED SALAD

The pulled pork popular in the South takes hours, even days to prepare—starting with digging a pit. Our barbecued pork has a similar flavor, but takes just minutes to make.

WINE RECOMMENDATION
With sweet, smoky-tasting barbecue, it's a toss-up between an exuberant Californian zinfandel and a lush, jammy Australian shiraz.

SERVES 4

2½ tablespoons wine vinegar

¼ tablespoon dried thyme

1¼ teaspoons salt

    Fresh-ground black pepper

¼ cup olive oil

1 pound pork tenderloin

2 tablespoons cooking oil

1 cup bottled barbecue sauce

½ teaspoon ground cumin

6 ounces cheddar or Monterey jack, shredded (about 1½ cups)

4 9-inch flour tortillas

½ head romaine lettuce, chopped (about 2 cups)

3 tomatoes, diced

2 green bell peppers, diced

1 cucumber, peeled, halved lengthwise, seeded, and diced

1. In a medium bowl, whisk 1½ tablespoons of the vinegar, the thyme, ¾ teaspoon of the salt, and ⅛ teaspoon pepper. Add the olive oil slowly, whisking.

2. Heat the oven to 350°. Cut the pork into ¼-inch slices, and then cut the slices into ¼-inch strips. In a large frying pan, heat 1 tablespoon of the cooking oil over high heat. Add half the pork, sprinkle with ¼ teaspoon of the salt, and sauté until cooked through and just beginning to brown, 3 to 4 minutes. Remove. Heat the remaining 1 tablespoon cooking oil and cook the rest of the pork, seasoning it with the remaining ¼ teaspoon salt.

3. Return all the pork to the pan. Stir in the barbecue sauce, cumin, the remaining 1 tablespoon vinegar, and two thirds (about 1 cup) of the cheese. Spread some of the pork mixture in a line just below the center of each tortilla. Roll up the burritos and put them seam-side down in a small baking dish. Bake for 10 minutes, sprinkle with the remaining cheese, and bake until the cheese melts and the filling is hot, about 2 minutes longer.

4. Meanwhile, put the lettuce, tomatoes, bell peppers, and cucumber into the bowl and toss. Put the salad on plates and top with the burritos.

SAUSAGE AND BLACK-BEAN BURRITOS

These overstuffed burritos need little adornment, but if you like, top each one with a dollop of salsa, or with some jicama cut into matchsticks and tossed with lime juice and chile powder. Whether plain or garnished, the hot burritos will be best with an extra squeeze of lime juice just before you dig in.

WINE RECOMMENDATION

Hot Italian sausage, black beans, tomato, and cheese all argue for a big, fruity red wine. Find a robust zinfandel from California; its blackberry flavor and intriguing woodsy quality will stand up to, and enhance, this dish.

SERVES 4

- ¾ pound hot Italian sausage, casings removed
- 1⅔ cups drained and rinsed canned black beans (one 15-ounce can)
- ¼ teaspoon salt
- ½ pound Monterey jack or cheddar, shredded (about 2 cups)
- 1 tomato, chopped
- 2 tablespoons lime juice (from about 1 lime)
- 1 red onion, chopped
- 4 9-inch flour tortillas
  Lime wedges, for serving

1. Heat the oven to 350°. In a large frying pan, cook the sausage over moderate heat, breaking it up with a fork or wooden spoon, until cooked through and just beginning to brown, about 10 minutes. Remove.

2. Pour off all but 1 tablespoon fat from the pan and reduce the heat to low. Add the beans and salt and cook, mashing the beans with the back of a wooden spoon, until heated through, 2 to 3 minutes. Most of the beans should be broken up, but don't mash them to a puree. Remove from the heat and stir in the sausage, half of the cheese, the tomato, lime juice, and onion.

3. Spread one quarter of the bean mixture in a line just below the center of each tortilla. Put the remaining cheese on top of the beans. Roll up the burritos and put them seam-side down in a small baking dish. Bake until the cheese is melted and the filling is hot, about 15 minutes. If the tops begin to brown too much, cover loosely with a sheet of aluminum foil. Serve the burritos with lime wedges.

VARIATION

Cut 1 pound of **bacon** crosswise into small strips. Fry until crisp and drain on paper towels. Proceed with the recipe from Step 2, substituting the bacon for the sausage.

FAJITAS WITH ROQUEFORT

Fajitas get a jolt of flavor when crumbled Roquefort replaces shredded cheddar or jack. You can roll the steak, onions, peppers, and cheese in the tortillas before serving, or put all the ingredients on the table and let people prepare their own.

WINE RECOMMENDATION

Fajitas and merlot go together like chips and salsa. The wine's plum, chocolate, and herb flavors are a natural with steak and peppers, while its soft, velvety texture plays counterpoint to the fajitas' rough-hewn construction.

SERVES 4

8	6-inch flour or corn tortillas
3	tablespoons cooking oil
2	onions, cut into thin slices
2	green bell peppers, cut into thin strips
1	teaspoon salt
1¼	pounds skirt steak, cut into 2 pieces
¼	teaspoon fresh-ground black pepper
¼	pound Roquefort or other blue cheese, crumbled (about 1 cup)

1. Heat the oven to 350°. Stack the tortillas and wrap them in aluminum foil. Warm in the oven for about 15 minutes.

2. In a large frying pan, heat 2 tablespoons of the oil over moderately high heat. Add the onions, peppers, and ½ teaspoon of the salt and cook, stirring occasionally, until browned, about 10 minutes. Set aside.

3. Light the grill or heat the broiler. Coat the steaks with the remaining 1 tablespoon oil. Sprinkle with the remaining ½ teaspoon salt and the black pepper. Grill or broil the steaks for 3 minutes. Turn the meat and cook to your taste, 2 to 3 minutes longer for medium rare. Let rest in a warm spot for 5 minutes. Cut the steaks diagonally across the grain into thin slices.

4. Roll the steak slices, onions and peppers, and Roquefort in the warm tortillas.

VARIATION

For a new-style **Philly cheese steak**, use the same filling, but put it in crusty rolls.

CHAPTER SEVEN

Salads

CAESAR SALAD WITH SHRIMP

Our modified Caesar dressing contains no egg, but tastes just as good as the original. This recipe can also be used to transform leftovers into a new meal. Substitute roast beef, chicken, cooked ham, or almost any meat, poultry, or fish you have for the shrimp.

WINE RECOMMENDATION

Dijon mustard, lemon, and sauvignon blanc combine in a way that makes them seem almost inseparable. A crisp Sancerre's vibrant gooseberry and lemon flavor, along with its strong chalky streak, will highlight the freshness of the salad and the sweetness of the shrimp.

SERVES 4

1   10-ounce loaf sourdough or country-style bread, cut into $3/4$-inch cubes (about 5 cups)

$3/4$ cup plus 2 tablespoons olive oil

4   tablespoons lemon juice

2   cloves garlic, chopped

$1/2$ cup grated Parmesan

1   teaspoon anchovy paste

2   teaspoons Dijon mustard

1   teaspoon salt

$1/2$ teaspoon fresh-ground black pepper

1   pound medium shrimp, shelled

1   head romaine lettuce, quartered lengthwise and cut crosswise into $1/2$-inch strips (about $1/2$ quarts)

2   cups halved cherry tomatoes

1. Heat the oven to 325°. Toss the bread cubes with 1 tablespoon of the oil and spread on a large baking sheet. Bake until crisp on the outside and lightly browned, about 15 minutes. Let cool.

2. Meanwhile, put the lemon juice, garlic, Parmesan, anchovy paste, mustard, $1/2$ teaspoon of the salt, and $1/4$ teaspoon of the pepper in a blender and blend until smooth. With the blender running, slowly add the $3/4$ cup oil. Alternatively, whisk together everything but the oil and then add the oil slowly, still whisking.

3. Heat the broiler. In a broiler pan or on a baking sheet, toss the shrimp with the remaining 1 tablespoon oil, $1/2$ teaspoon salt, and $1/4$ teaspoon pepper. Broil the shrimp, turning once, until just done, about 4 minutes in all.

4. In a large bowl, combine the lettuce, tomatoes, croutons, and shrimp. Add the dressing and toss to coat.

TUNA, CHICKPEA, FENNEL, AND ORANGE SALAD

Canned tuna has never been better than in this salad—where it's combined with a delightful array of flavors, from mild chickpeas to sweet oranges to fiery jalapeño. We like to cut the orange sections away from the membranes, but if you're in hurry, just slice the oranges.

WINE RECOMMENDATION
Instead of the more traditional riesling, accompany this tuna with a Pfalz spätlese made from scheurebe. The wine's wild, even exotic scents of grapefruit, orange peel, minerals, and flint will be a pleasant and harmonious surprise.

SERVES 4

¼ cup lemon juice

1 teaspoon Dijon mustard

1½ teaspoons salt

½ teaspoon fresh-ground black pepper

½ cup olive oil

2 6-ounce cans tuna packed in oil, drained

2 cups drained and rinsed chickpeas (one 19-ounce can)

2 navel oranges

½ head romaine lettuce, cut into 1-inch pieces (about 3 cups)

1 large fennel bulb, cut into quarters and then into thin slices

1 red onion, chopped

1 jalapeño pepper, seeds and ribs removed, minced

⅓ cup chopped cilantro (optional)

1. In a large glass or stainless-steel bowl, whisk together the lemon juice, mustard, salt, and pepper. Add the oil slowly, whisking.

2. In a medium glass or stainless-steel bowl, combine the tuna and chickpeas. Gently stir in ¼ cup of the dressing.

3. Using a stainless-steel knife, peel the oranges down to the flesh, removing all of the white pith. Cut the sections away from the membranes and set aside. Squeeze 2 tablespoons of the juice from the membranes into the remaining dressing.

4. Add the tuna and chickpeas, orange sections, lettuce, fennel, onion, jalapeño, and cilantro to the dressing and toss gently.

CHICKEN AND BULGUR SALAD WITH CORN

Bulgur makes a hearty base for a salad. Here, it's tossed with corn kernels, tomato, red onion, and a bit of hot pepper, dressed with lime vinaigrette, and then topped with slices of sautéed chicken breast for an ideal summer meal.

WINE RECOMMENDATION
German rieslings show their great adaptability by flattering notoriously difficult-to-match salads. The earthy flavors of a young Pfalz spätlese will match those of the sweet corn and chicken.

SERVES 4

2/3 cup bulgur

2/3 cup boiling water

4½ tablespoons olive oil

4 cups fresh (cut from about 6 ears) or frozen corn kernels

1½ teaspoons salt

1 small red onion, chopped

1⅓ pounds boneless skinless chicken breasts (about 4)

¼ teaspoon fresh-ground black pepper

1 tomato, seeded and chopped

1 jalapeño pepper, seeds and ribs removed, minced

½ cup chopped cilantro (optional)

4 tablespoons lime juice (from about 2 limes)

¼ teaspoon cayenne

1. In a medium bowl, combine the bulgur and the water. Cover and let sit for 20 minutes.

2. In a large nonstick frying pan, heat 1½ tablespoons of the oil over moderate heat. Add the corn and ¼ teaspoon of the salt and cook, stirring occasionally, for 5 minutes. Add the onion and continue cooking for 5 minutes longer, stirring occasionally. Transfer to a large glass or stainless-steel bowl and let cool.

3. Add 1 tablespoon of the oil to the frying pan and heat over moderate heat. Season the chicken with ¼ teaspoon of the salt and the black pepper. Cook the breasts until browned and just done, about 5 minutes per side. Remove the chicken from the pan and let it rest for 5 minutes. Cut crosswise into ¼-inch slices.

4. Add the bulgur, tomato, jalapeño, cilantro, 3 tablespoons of the lime juice, the cayenne, and ¾ teaspoon of the salt to the bowl with the corn and onion. Toss.

5. In a small glass or stainless-steel bowl, combine the remaining 1 tablespoon lime juice, 2 tablespoons oil, and ¼ teaspoon salt. Mound the salad onto plates. Top with the chicken and drizzle the chicken with the lime oil.

CHICKEN AND RICE SALAD WITH PINE NUTS AND LEMON

We like to serve this Mediterranean-inspired salad warm, but it's also good slightly chilled. Be sure to check the seasonings, though; cold dishes often need more salt and pepper than those served hot.

WINE RECOMMENDATION
The ingredients may call to mind the Mediterranean, but this salad will really sing with a dry riesling from Alsace in northern France. The wine's cleansing acidity and delicate taste of citrus and peach will both mirror and contrast the flavors and textures here perfectly.

SERVES 4

¼ cup pine nuts

¼ cup plus 1 tablespoon lemon juice (from about 2 lemons)

Salt

Fresh-ground black pepper

½ cup plus 2 tablespoons olive oil

1½ cups frozen petite peas

2 cups long-grain rice

1⅓ pounds boneless skinless chicken breasts (about 4)

¼ cup plus 2 tablespoons golden raisins

6 scallions including green tops, chopped

3 tablespoons minced flat-leaf parsley

1½ teaspoons grated lemon zest

1. In a small frying pan, toast the pine nuts over moderately low heat, stirring frequently, until they are golden brown, about 5 minutes. Or toast the pine nuts in a 350° oven for about 8 minutes.

2. In a small glass or stainless-steel bowl, whisk together the lemon juice, 1 teaspoon salt, and ¼ teaspoon pepper. Add the oil slowly, whisking.

3. Bring a large pot of salted water to a boil. Add the peas; cook until just barely tender, about 3 minutes. Using a slotted spoon or a strainer, transfer to a large bowl. Add the rice to the water and cook until tender, about 15 minutes. Drain, return to the pot, and cover to keep warm.

4. Meanwhile, in a large frying pan, bring ¼ inch of water to a simmer over moderately high heat. Sprinkle the chicken with salt and pepper and add to the pan. Cover, reduce the heat, and simmer, turning once, until cooked through, about 12 minutes. Remove the chicken, let cool slightly, and then cut into approximately ½-inch chunks.

5. Add the pine nuts, rice, chicken, raisins, scallions, parsley, lemon zest, and dressing to the large bowl and stir gently to mix.

PERSIAN CHICKEN SALAD

Traditionally, Persian salads are decked with a variety of fresh herbs, such as mint, basil, and parsley. You may want to add some sprigs to garnish this version; the leaves can be eaten right along with the salad. Hot pita is an ideal accompaniment.

WINE RECOMMENDATION
Pouilly-Fumé is a can't-miss partner for fresh herbs and vegetables. Made from sauvignon blanc in France's Loire Valley, Pouilly-Fumé has penetrating herbal flavors of its own.

SERVES 4

1½ pounds small new potatoes (about 6), cut into quarters

3 tablespoons olive oil

1⅓ pounds boneless skinless chicken breasts (about 4)

1½ teaspoons salt

½ teaspoon fresh-ground black pepper

1 cup plain yogurt

½ cup mayonnaise

1 tablespoon Dijon mustard

¼ cup lime juice (from about 2 limes)

4 carrots, grated

2 cucumbers, peeled, halved, seeded, and cut into ¼-inch dice

2 ribs celery, cut into ¼-inch dice

1 cup frozen petite peas, thawed

1 red onion, chopped fine

½ cup Kalamata or other black olives, halved and pitted

⅓ cup chopped flat-leaf parsley

½ cup chopped fresh basil or parsley

1. Put the potatoes in a medium saucepan of salted water. Bring to a boil, reduce the heat, and simmer until just tender, about 12 minutes. Drain the potatoes and let cool.

2. In a large nonstick frying pan, heat 1 tablespoon of the oil over moderate heat. Season the chicken with ¼ teaspoon each of the salt and pepper. Cook the breasts until browned and just done, about 5 minutes per side. Remove the chicken from the pan and let it cool. Cut into ½-inch chunks.

3. In a large glass or stainless-steel bowl, whisk together the yogurt, mayonnaise, mustard, lime juice, and the remaining 1¼ teaspoons salt and ¼ teaspoon pepper. Add the potatoes, chicken, carrots, cucumbers, celery, peas, onion, olives, parsley, and basil and toss.

PARMESAN-POLENTA-COATED CHICKEN LIVERS WITH LENTIL SALAD

Lovers of chicken livers will find this dish a treat, and we think even those who are skeptical will fall for these morsels with their crisp coating and subtle cheese flavor.

WINE RECOMMENDATION
The creamy rich livers and the crunchy dressed salad both call for a tart, fruity red wine. A Beaujolais will be an ideal accompaniment.

SERVES 4

1	pound lentils (about 2⅓ cups)
1	quart water
1	onion, chopped fine
2	cloves garlic, minced
2¾	teaspoons salt
2½	tablespoons sherry vinegar or wine vinegar
1½	teaspoons Dijon mustard
½	teaspoon fresh-ground black pepper
½	cup plus 2 tablespoons olive oil
2	tomatoes, chopped
⅓	cup chopped flat-leaf parsley
½	cup coarse cornmeal
½	cup grated Parmesan
2	eggs, beaten to mix
2	tablespoons butter
1	pound chicken livers
2	quarts mixed salad greens (about 6 ounces)

1. In a large saucepan, combine the lentils, water, onion, garlic, and 1½ teaspoons of the salt. Bring to a boil, reduce the heat, and simmer, partially covered, until the lentils are just tender but not falling apart, about 35 minutes. Drain and transfer to a large bowl to cool.

2. In a large glass or stainless-steel bowl, whisk together the vinegar, mustard, ¾ teaspoon of the salt, and ¼ teaspoon of the pepper. Add the ½ cup oil slowly, whisking. Add ½ cup of this vinaigrette to the lentil salad along with the tomatoes and parsley.

3. In a shallow dish, combine the cornmeal, Parmesan, and the remaining ½ teaspoon salt and ¼ teaspoon pepper. Put the eggs in another shallow dish. In a large nonstick frying pan, heat 1 tablespoon of the oil and 1 tablespoon of the butter over moderate heat. Dip half the livers in the egg and then into the cornmeal mixture; fry for 2 minutes. Turn and cook until browned but still pink inside, about 2 minutes longer. Repeat with the remaining livers and the remaining 1 tablespoon each oil and butter.

4. To serve, toss the greens in the remaining vinaigrette and put on plates. Top with the lentils and livers.

GREEK SALAD WITH PEPPERONI

Pepperoni—sliced thin, sautéed until crisp—is a tempting addition to this traditional combination of greens, vegetables, and feta cheese and makes the salad substantial enough for dinner.

WINE RECOMMENDATION
Usually salads call for white wines, the crisper and fruitier the better, but the pepperoni here points toward a red. Italy's Bardolino or Valpolicella will work well.

SERVES 4

¼ pound thin-sliced pepperoni, slices cut in half

¼ cup lemon juice (from about 1 lemon)

1 teaspoon dried oregano

¾ teaspoon salt

¼ teaspoon fresh-ground black pepper

½ cup olive oil

1 large head romaine lettuce, cut into bite-size pieces (about 1½ quarts)

1 English cucumber, halved lengthwise and cut into thin slices

3 tomatoes, cut into wedges

1 red onion, cut into thin slices

1 green bell pepper, cut into ½-inch pieces

¾ cup Kalamata olives, pitted

8 ounces feta, crumbled (about 1½ cups)

1. In a large frying pan, cook the pepperoni over moderate heat, stirring occasionally, until lightly browned, about 3 minutes. Drain.

2. In a large glass or stainless-steel bowl, whisk the lemon juice, oregano, salt, and black pepper. Add the oil slowly, whisking. Add the lettuce, cucumber, tomatoes, onion, bell pepper, olives, cheese, and pepperoni and toss to coat.

TEST-KITCHEN TIP

Using an English, or hothouse, cucumber—the long and skinny kind sold in shrink-wrap—eliminates the need for peeling and seeding. You can substitute two regular cucumbers for the one English cucumber here, but they should be peeled, halved lengthwise, seeded, and sliced. Likewise, you can replace the seeded cucumbers in any of our recipes with English.

BREAD SALAD WITH FONTINA AND BLACK-FOREST HAM

A cross between *panzanella* (Italian bread salad) and an upscale chef's salad, this recipe calls for more croutons than lettuce and incorporates cubes of fontina and strips of silky cured ham. Use either a mild Dutch or Danish fontina or a more assertive Italian cheese, depending on your taste.

WINE RECOMMENDATION
This full-flavored salad can easily partner a red wine—even, because of its ham and cheese, one with some tannin. A Beaujolais-Villages, light-bodied, fruity, and just a bit tannic, will be delicious.

SERVES 4

1   10-ounce loaf country-style bread, cut into 1-inch cubes (about 5 cups)

⅔   cup plus 3 tablespoons olive oil

¼   cup plus 1 tablespoon red-wine vinegar

1   clove garlic, minced

¾   teaspoon salt

¼   teaspoon fresh-ground black pepper

½   pound fontina, cut into ½-inch cubes

2   cups halved cherry tomatoes

1   rib celery, sliced

1   small red onion, chopped

¼   cup minced fresh parsley

½   head romaine lettuce, cut into bite-size pieces (about 3 cups)

6   ounces sliced Black Forest ham, cut into strips approximately 1½ by ½ inch

1. Heat the oven to 325°. Toss the bread cubes with the 3 tablespoons oil and spread on a large baking sheet. Bake, stirring once or twice, until crisp and lightly browned on the outside but still soft inside, about 15 minutes. Let cool.

2. In a large glass or stainless-steel bowl, whisk the vinegar, garlic, salt, and pepper. Add the remaining ⅔ cup oil slowly, whisking.

3. Add the toasted bread, cheese, tomatoes, celery, onion, and parsley and toss to coat. Let sit for 5 minutes. Add the lettuce and ham and toss again.

Roast-Beef and Broccoli Salad with Creamy Horseradish Dressing

Horseradish cream is a traditional accompaniment to roast beef, hot or cold. Here roast beef from the deli is tossed with broccoli, cherry tomatoes, and a creamy horseradish dressing. We use the broccoli stems as well as the florets. When peeled they're as good as the tops—maybe better.

WINE RECOMMENDATION
White wine may seem an odd choice for roast beef, but the dominant elements here are horseradish and broccoli, not meat. Accordingly, pull the cork on a California sauvignon blanc for an exciting pairing.

SERVES 4

1½ pounds broccoli

2 tablespoons white-wine vinegar

¼ cup drained bottled horseradish

2 teaspoons Dijon mustard

¾ teaspoon salt

⅛ teaspoon fresh-ground black pepper

½ cup olive or other oil

3 tablespoons sour cream

¾ pound thick-sliced (⅛ inch) roast beef, cut crosswise into ½-inch strips

2½ cups halved cherry tomatoes

6 scallions including green tops, cut diagonally into thin slices

1. Separate the broccoli tops into small florets. Peel the broccoli stems and cut them in half lengthwise and then into ¼-inch slices. In a large saucepan, steam or boil the broccoli until tender, 4 to 5 minutes. Drain and let cool.

2. In a large glass or stainless-steel bowl, whisk together the vinegar, horseradish, mustard, salt, and pepper. Add the oil slowly, whisking. Whisk in the sour cream. Add the broccoli, beef, tomatoes, and scallions and toss to coat.

LAMB FATTOUSH

Tomatoes, cucumber, green pepper, and mint are tossed with torn and toasted pitas and topped with grilled butterflied leg of lamb for a delectable Middle Eastern salad. If you can't find a one-and-a-half-pound piece of leg of lamb, substitute lamb steaks and grill or broil them for about five minutes a side. Don't add the pitas until you're ready to serve the salad, or they will get soggy.

WINE RECOMMENDATION
The great red wines of the Loire Valley are made almost exclusively from cabernet franc, which imbues them with strawberry aromas, cassis and berry flavors, and a distinct leafy note. It all adds up to a fabulous match for this salad. Go for a young Saumur-Champigny or Chinon.

SERVES 4

3 pitas, torn into 1-inch pieces

1½ pounds butterflied leg of lamb

⅓ cup plus 1 tablespoon olive oil

1 teaspoon salt

½ teaspoon fresh-ground black pepper

5 tablespoons lemon juice (from about 2 lemons)

3 cloves garlic, minced

1 pound tomatoes (about 2 large), cut into ½-inch dice

1 cucumber, peeled, halved, seeded, and cut into ½-inch dice

1 green bell pepper, cut into ½-inch dice

6 scallions including green tops, cut into thin slices

1 small red onion, chopped

½ cup chopped fresh mint

¼ cup chopped flat-leaf parsley

1. Heat the oven to 375°. Put the pitas in a single layer on a baking sheet and toast in the oven until brown, about 12 minutes. Let cool.

2. Light a grill or heat the broiler. Coat the lamb with the 1 tablespoon oil and season with ¼ teaspoon of the salt and ¼ teaspoon of the black pepper. Grill over moderate heat for 10 minutes. Turn and cook until done to your taste, about 10 minutes longer, depending on the thickness, for medium rare. Alternatively, broil the meat, 6 inches from the heat if possible, for the same amount of time. Transfer the lamb to a carving board and let rest for 10 minutes. Carve into thin slices against the grain.

3. Meanwhile, in a large glass or stainless-steel bowl, whisk together the lemon juice, garlic, and the remaining ¾ teaspoon salt and ¼ teaspoon black pepper. Add the ⅓ cup oil slowly, whisking. Add the tomatoes, cucumber, bell pepper, scallions, onion, mint, parsley, and pitas. Serve topped with the lamb.

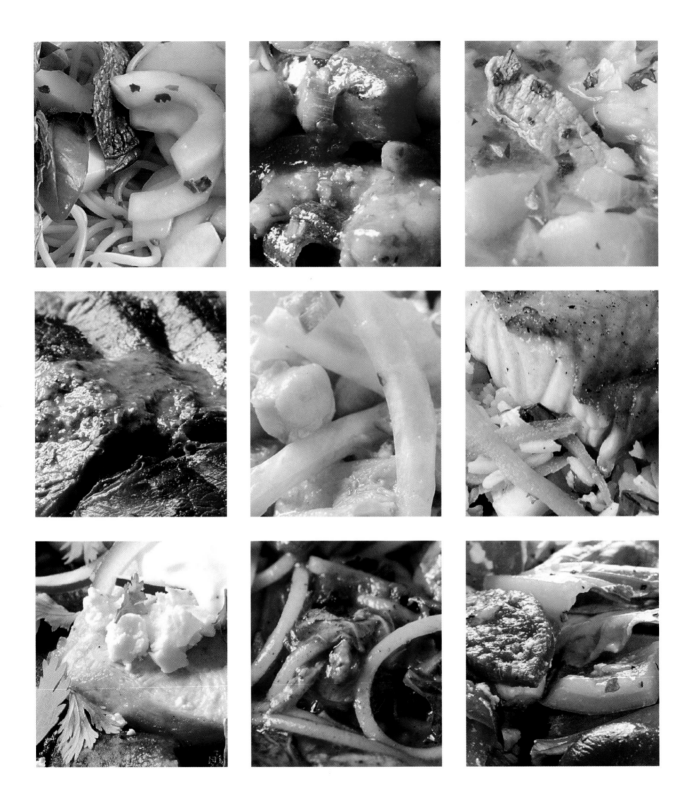

Planning Your Quick Meals

Look to this section for practical help in deciding what ingredients to keep on hand, what dish to make, and what simple wine to serve with it. Among the useful guides, you'll find ideas for seasonal meals and a list of recipes in which you can include leftovers.

THE QUICK PANTRY

If you keep staple ingredients on hand, you'll only have to make one short stop to pick up the fresh vegetables, meat, poultry, or seafood you need to complete the recipe.

CUPBOARD

- beans, canned: black, cannellini, chickpeas
- bread crumbs
- bulgur
- chicken broth, low-sodium
- clam juice, bottled
- coconut milk, unsweetened
- cornmeal
- couscous
- garlic
- lentils
- oil: cooking, olive
- onions
- pasta, dried
- peppers, bottled
- pimientos
- potatoes
- raisins
- rice: arborio, basmati, long grain
- soy sauce
- Tabasco sauce
- tomatoes: canned, paste, sun-dried
- tortilla chips
- tuna, oil-packed
- vinegar: red- or white-wine, sherry

LIQUOR CABINET

- beer
- bourbon
- brandy
- sake
- sherry
- vermouth, dry
- wine: dry white, red

SPICE SHELF

- allspice
- bay leaves
- cardamom, ground
- cayenne
- chili powder
- cinnamon, ground and sticks
- cloves
- cocoa powder
- coriander, ground
- cumin
- dill
- nutmeg
- oregano
- paprika
- red-pepper flakes
- rosemary
- sage
- thyme
- turmeric

FREEZER

- bacon
- nuts: cashews, peanuts, pine nuts
- pasta: cavatelli, tortellini
- pizza dough
- vegetables: corn, lima beans, okra, peas

REFRIGERATOR

- anchovy paste
- barbecue sauce
- butter
- capers
- cheese: cream, fontina, goat, mozzarella, Parmesan
- cilantro
- cream
- curry paste, red
- eggs
- fish sauce, Asian
- ginger, fresh
- horseradish, bottled
- jalapeño peppers
- ketchup
- lemons
- limes
- mayonnaise
- milk
- mustard: Dijon or grainy
- olives: black, green
- oranges
- oyster sauce
- parsley
- pesto
- pizza shells, prepared
- scallions
- sesame oil, Asian
- sour cream
- tofu
- tortillas: corn, flour
- yogurt, plain

RECIPES PICTURED OPPOSITE: (top) pages 29, 115, 83; (center) pages 111, 161, 45; (bottom) pages 123, 75, 171

EVERYDAY WINES

by Steve Miller

Some people may feel that wine is for special occasions only, reserved for Saturday nights, elaborate dinners, and holiday family gatherings. But wine can be an integral part of our everyday lives, and I can hardly imagine even the simplest weekday supper without its enlivening savor. I'm not talking about profound wines, however. To drink the great classics every evening would surely be as tiring as nightly indulgence in rich Escoffier cuisine. Not to mention devastating to the bank account.

What we need for everyday consumption are good, reliable wines that are affordable and widely available. With rare exceptions, the wines I have recommended in this book should require no more than a five minute stop at your favorite wineshop on the way home from work. None of them should top $20, with the vast majority selling for well under $10. To save more time and money, consider buying the ones you like best by the case.

As you read through the recipes and their accompanying wine recommendations, you may be struck by the simplicity of many of the selections. One-dish meals are often exciting mélanges of ingredients that result in complex flavors and textures. It is almost always best to highlight such dishes with uncomplicated and fruity wines that act as a backdrop, rather than complex ones that vie with the food for center stage. Thus you will see some familiar, versatile staples of the wine world show up again and again.

But what if you happen not to like the wine I have suggested? Or if you're just dying to try something else you are convinced will work better with the recipe at hand? Don't worry. While I feel that each of these food-and-wine pairings will be delicious, they are suggestions only. I encourage you to experiment on your own. Use these recommendations as starting points, and then trust your own taste.

Steve Miller is a wine consultant, educator, and writer. He regularly contributes to the Wine Enthusiast.

SEASONAL DISHES

So many fresh vegetables and herbs are now available throughout the year that you can make most of our recipes any time you like. Nevertheless, some produce is still better and cheaper in a particular season. It's hard, for instance, to capture the full flavor of a pasta sauce made with fresh tomatoes and basil in any season but summer. And even if the ingredients involved are of good quality year-round, some dishes just taste better in a certain season, such as hearty stews in winter and cool salads in the warm summer months. Here are our suggestions for those times when you want to cook in tune with the season.

Spring

- Asparagus Risotto with Crab and Orange Gremolada, *page 41*
- Rice with Mozzarella, Prosciutto, and Peas, *page 51*
- Shrimp with Minty Couscous Salad, *page 57*
- Roasted Chicken, New Potatoes, and Asparagus, *page 95*

Summer

- Whole-Wheat Pasta with Tofu and Cucumber, *page 17*
- Spaghetti with Grilled Shrimp, Zucchini, and Salsa Verde, *page 21*
- Salmon with Thai Rice Salad, *page 45*
- Swordfish with Vegetable Couscous and Tomato Vinaigrette, *page 59*
- Flank Steak with Corn-Kernel Polenta, *page 65*
- Pasta Salad with Seared Tuna and Citrus Dressing, *page 121*
- Summer Pizza, *page 139*
- Tuna, Chickpea, Fennel, and Orange Salad, *page 161*
- Chicken and Bulgur Salad with Corn, *page 163*
- Lamb Fattoush, *page 177*

Fall

- Orzo with Chicken, Red Pepper, and Shiitakes, *page 27*
- Turkey and Sweet-Potato Soup, *page 79*
- Roasted Salmon, Beets, and Potatoes with Horseradish Cream, *page 93*
- Pork Chops with Mushroom Bread Pudding, *page 97*
- Grilled Spice-Rubbed Pork Tenderloin, Sweet Potatoes, and Scallions, *page 109*
- Scallop-Topped Potato and Celery-Root Puree with Lemon Brown-Butter Sauce, *page 117*

Winter

- Country-Style Rigatoni, *page 31*
- Baked Shells with Pesto, Mozzarella, and Meat Sauce, *page 37*
- Sausage and Broccoli Rabe with Polenta, *page 63*
- Gingered Cabbage Soup with Pork and Potatoes, *page 83*
- Lentils with Smoked Sausage and Carrots, *page 129*

LEFTOVERS

Think of leftovers as a head start; they're the original timesavers. Listed here are the recipes in this book that use cooked poultry, meat, or fish, for which precooked ingredients would be fine. You might even plan to roast a little extra chicken or beef with Sunday's dinner to save yourself a step later in the week. We also list recipes to which you could add leftovers to make a slightly different dish that is at least as good as the original.

Fish

Substitute leftover shellfish or finfish in:
• Spaghetti with Grilled Shrimp, Zucchini, and Salsa Verde, *page 21*
• Linguine with Scallops, Sun-Dried Tomatoes, and Pine Nuts, *page 23*
• Asparagus Risotto with Crab and Orange Gremolada, *page 41*
• Dirty Rice with Shrimp, *page 43*
• Salmon with Thai Rice Salad, *page 45*
• Shrimp with Minty Couscous Salad, *page 57*
• Swordfish with Vegetable Couscous and Tomato Vinaigrette, *page 59*
• Salmon-and-Corn Chowder with Lima Beans, *page 71*
• Shellfish Stew with Chorizo and Rouille, *page 85*
• Red Snapper on Rice with Red-Curry Carrot Sauce, *page 119*
• Pasta Salad with Seared Tuna and Citrus Dressing, *page 121*
• Caesar Salad with Shrimp, *page 159*

Add leftover shellfish or finfish to:
• Whole-Wheat Pasta with Tofu and Cucumber, *page 17*
• Summer Pizza, *page 139*

Poultry

Substitute leftover cooked chicken or turkey in:
• Orzo with Chicken, Red Pepper, and Shiitakes, *page 27*
• Vermicelli with Chicken Skewers and Nuoc Cham, *page 29*
• Indonesian Coconut Rice with Chicken and Zucchini, *page 47*
• Tortilla Soup, *page 73*
• Asian Chicken Noodle Soup, *page 75*
• Chicken and Smoked-Sausage Gumbo, *page 77*
• Turkey and Sweet-Potato Soup, *page 79*
• Turkey and Black-Bean Soup, *page 81*
• Chicken Chilaquiles, *page 123*
• Chicken and Bulgur Salad with Corn, *page 163*
• Chicken and Rice Salad with Pine Nuts and Lemon, *page 165*
• Persian Chicken Salad, *page 167*

Add leftover chicken or turkey to:
• Whole-Wheat Pasta with Tofu and Cucumber, *page 17*

Pork

Substitute leftover pork roast or chops in:
- Gingered Cabbage Soup with Pork and Potatoes, *page 83*
- Barbecued-Pork Burritos with Chopped Salad, *page 151*

Substitute leftover cooked sausage in:
- Country-Style Rigatoni, *page 31*
- Sun-Dried-Tomato, Sausage, and Fontina Pizza, *page 143*
- Sausage and Black-Bean Burritos, *page 153*

Add salami or pepperoni to:
- Fusilli with Three Cheeses and Red Bell Pepper, *page 19*
- Summer Pizza, *page 139*

Beef

Substitute leftover roast beef or steak in:
- Beef Fried Rice, *page 53*
- Grilled Steak over Black Beans with Chimichurri Sauce, *page 111*
- Fajitas with Roquefort, *page 155*
- Roast-Beef and Broccoli Salad with Creamy Horseradish Dressing, *page 175*

Lamb

Substitute leftover roast lamb or chops in:
- Lamb Chops with Tomato-and-Potato Gratin, *page 103*
- Lamb Fattoush, *page 177*

INDEX

Page numbers in **boldface** indicate photographs   ❦ indicates wine recommendations